T0246293

PRAISE FOR
THINK FASTER, TALK SMARTER

● ● ●

"Being able to speak confidently off the cuff impacts every facet of our lives. Matt Abrahams has spent decades developing tools that harness the power of spontaneous communication, and not just for public speakers but for anyone who finds themselves needing to speak in the moment. *Think Faster, Talk Smarter* provides you with easy-to-implement, actionable tips and techniques for success." —Philip Zimbardo, psychology professor emeritus Stanford University and author of *The Lucifer Effect* and *Living and Loving Better with Time Perspective Therapy*

"*Think Faster, Talk Smarter* is just the book you need to improve at spontaneous public speaking. Matt Abrahams offers a six-step approach to help anyone think faster and talk smarter when put on the spot. Grounded in careful research and informed by Abrahams's many years teaching communication skills to Stanford MBAs, this book is filled with useful advice." —Katy Milkman author of *How to Change: The Science of Getting from Where You Are to Where You Want to Be* and host of the *Choiceology* podcast

"Matt's ideas and insights in *Think Faster, Talk Smarter* are priceless. I spent my life working in front of a television camera but would get nervous speaking in front of a live crowd. That would shock people since millions saw me every day—but of course, I didn't see them. It took me years to conquer my nerves and feel comfortable and confident speaking in front of a live audience. Matt makes it easy with his focus on the connection over perfection. His specific examples in the book provide a clear road map to help you be your best self when under pressure." —Joan Lunden, journalist, author, keynote speaker, and television host

"We read the book and now we're furiously fast, shockingly smart. Matt blends wit with wisdom and science-backed strategies with actionable insights, empowering us all to communicate with greater confidence and connection. Plus, it's a joy to read."—Jennifer Aaker and Naomi Bagdonas authors of *Humor, Seriously: Why Humor Is a Secret Weapon in Business and Life (And how anyone can harness it. Even you.)*

"Want to ace that interview? Win over a new customer? Look smart in meetings? *Think Faster, Talk Smarter* will teach you how to shine in those moments instead of dreading them. The book is chock-full of exercises that will help you cope with one of life's trickiest situations— when you're put on the spot and need to come up with something intelligent to say. The most intelligent thing I can say right now is, read this book!" —Dan Lyons, journalist, satirist, and author of *Disrupted, Lab Rats,* and *STFU: The Power of Keeping Your Mouth Shut in an Endlessly Noisy World*

"Where was Matt Abrahams when I started my media career? The steps that he outlines in *Think Faster, Talk Smarter* have taken me decades to master! Luckily for everyone else, his guide to mastering impromptu speaking can speed up the process with smart, actionable tactics that will help you overcome your fears and anxieties and communicate with ease and confidence." —Jill Schlesinger, CBS News business analyst and author of *The Great Money Reset*

"Salivate. Dare to be dull. Turn resistance into curiosity. Every page of Matt Abrahams's relentlessly useful and entertaining gem is packed with research-based ideas about how all of us anxious speakers can banish our fears, harness our anxiety, and persuade audiences to appreciate us and our ideas. My only complaint is that I wish I had read it twenty years ago!" —Robert I. Sutton, *New York Times* bestselling author of eight books, including *The No Asshole Rule, Scaling Up Excellence* (with Huggy Rao), and *The Friction Project* (with Huggy Rao)

"*Think Faster, Talk Smarter* serves as a gold standard for communication best practices. Matt's six-step approach to speaking confidently and clearly in spontaneous situations helps calm the nervous system so you can focus on what matters: creating connection with those around you and responding in the moment. If you struggle with any type of communication, this book is for you."—David Eagleman, neuroscientist, author, technologist, entrepreneur, and host of the *Inner Cosmos with David Eagleman* podcast

"Being able to communicate a creative vision to teams both small and large is crucial to being successful. In *Think Faster, Talk Smarter*, Matt has broken down the elements that go into becoming a more successful communicator. His clear approach, along with relatable and actionable examples, can help anyone feel better about impromptu speaking no matter what the situation. I highly recommend anyone who wants to improve their communication skills read *Think Faster, Talk Smarter*." —John Janick, chairman and CEO of Interscope Geffen A&M Records

"Matt's understanding of human interaction is exceptional. His tools for thinking quickly and speaking clearly are indispensable for anyone, even in our modern texting world. His easy-to-understand approach helps anyone to become a better in-the-moment communicator." — Tony Fadell, Nest founder, iPod inventor, and *New York Times* best-selling author of *Build*

"In *Think Faster, Talk Smarter*, Matt Abrahams gives you the tools to build supreme confidence in your ability to sell your ideas, even in the most pressure-filled moments. I've followed Matt's work at Stanford Business School and in his inspiring TED talks. Now everyone can reap the benefit of Matt's experience as a leading communication expert. Don't let another opportunity to share your ideas go to waste—take Matt's advice to stand out and get ahead!" — Carmine Gallo, author, *Talk Like TED* and *The Bezos Blueprint*

"It's one thing to deliver a good speech; another entirely to be brilliant in the melée of spontaneous, unprepared conversation. Matt Abrahams is that rare thing: an academic who really knows his topic (communication skills) and can teach it in simple, practical and invaluable lessons that anyone can put to use straight away. This is an essential book for anyone who wants to communicate better." —Julian Treasure, author of *How To Be Heard* and *Sound Business*, and five-time TED speaker

THINK FASTER

FASTER

• • •

TALK SMARTER

HOW TO SPEAK SUCCESSFULLY
WHEN YOU'RE PUT ON THE SPOT

MATT ABRAHAMS

SIMON ELEMENT
New York   London   Toronto   Sydney   New Delhi

For all of my family, teachers, mentors, and collaborators.

You have helped me to think faster and talk smarter.

SIMON
ELEMENT

An Imprint of Simon & Schuster, Inc.
1230 Avenue of the Americas
New York, NY 10020

First Simon Element hardcover edition September 2023

SIMON ELEMENT is a trademark of Simon & Schuster, Inc.

For information about special discounts for bulk purchases, please contact
Simon & Schuster Special Sales at 1-866-506-1949 or business@simonandschuster.com.

The Simon & Schuster Speakers Bureau can bring authors to your live event. For more
information or to book an event, contact the Simon & Schuster Speakers Bureau at
1-866-248-3049 or visit our website at www.simonspeakers.com.

Interior design by Laura Levatino

Manufactured in the United States of America

10 9 8 7

Library of Congress Cataloging-in-Publication Data
Names: Abrahams, Matt, author.
Title: Think faster, talk smarter : how to speak successfully when you're
   put on the spot / Matt Abrahams.
Description: First Simon Element hardcover edition. | New York : Simon
   Element, 2023. | Includes bibliographical references and index. |
Identifiers: LCCN 2023020647 | ISBN 9781668010303 (hardcover) | ISBN
   9781668010310 (paperback) | ISBN 9781668010327 (ebook)
Subjects: LCSH: Extemporaneous speaking. | Speech anxiety.
Classification: LCC PN4168 .A27 2023 | DDC 808.35/1--dc23/eng/20230612
LC record available at https://lccn.loc.gov/2023020647

ISBN 978-1-6680-1030-3
ISBN 978-1-6680-1032-7 (ebook)

There is no greater agony than bearing an untold story inside you.

— Maya Angelou

It usually takes me more than three weeks

to prepare a good impromptu speech.

— Mark Twain

CONTENTS

INTRODUCTION

"What do *you* think?"

We've all been put on the spot with this simple, seemingly innocuous question. As others in the room wait for our response, we feel awkward, anxious, maybe even downright terrified.

Consider how you might feel if "What do *you* think" were . . .

- lobbed at you by your boss in a crowded Zoom meeting, at a moment when you're more interested in your lunch tacos than the topic at hand.
- uttered by a colleague in an elevator's cramped confines as you're leaving a big presentation they just gave that went horribly.
- posed by a senior executive interviewing you for an attractive job, as you dine with them and a half dozen members of their team.
- directed at you by an esteemed professor who has called on you at random in a large lecture hall.

Such sudden, unexpected queries put us on the spot and intimidate us. We feel pressed to respond quickly, clearly, and with at least a small dose of charm. Most of all, we want to avoid falling on our faces and embarrassing ourselves.

Let's be honest: What we're *really* thinking when people spring a question like this on us is, *THIS SUCKS!*

Spontaneous Communication? Or *Combustion?*

The need to speak spontaneously crops up many times in everyday life, often without someone explicitly asking us what we think. We're at a wedding reception and a friend calls us up to give a toast. We log in to a virtual meeting and find ourselves alone, face-to-face with the CEO, who wishes to strike up a conversation. We're at a swanky cocktail party and a colleague introduces us to a potentially important business contact. We're giving a formal presentation and the moderator asks if we might stick around for fifteen minutes of informal question and answer.

At still other times, we thrust ourselves into precarious situations in which we must think on our feet. We make an embarrassing faux pas and have to talk our way out of it. The technology we're relying on during an important pitch fails and we have to wing it. We say something we regret in a moment of frustration and must find a way to apologize. We experience a bout of "mental flatulence" and utterly forget someone's name or a point we were about to make.

For large numbers of us, the prospect of spontaneous communication is terrifying. Research has found that Americans fear public speaking more than they do bugs, heights, needles, zombies, ghosts, darkness, and clowns.[1] And that's formal, pre-planned public speaking. As research shows, impromptu speaking can freak us out even more, since we haven't had a chance to prepare and lack a script or outline to fall back on.[2]

Even those us who don't experience much anxiety when speaking publicly likely feel haunted by occasions when we misspoke, fumbled an answer, or failed to impress in a spontaneous speaking situation. Frustration over our lack of skill in these situations is as common as anxiety about future impromptu interactions. Both can derail our best-laid plans for presenting ourselves as the polished, passionate, responsive communicators we hope to be.

Blinded by the (Spot) Light

I'd like you to try something. Cross your arms in front of you as you normally would. Now, uncross them and cross them again, this time folding the other arm on top. Notice how weird this feels. For a split second, you're not quite sure what to do with your arms. Your mind becomes detached from your body and you feel confused, uncertain, maybe just a tiny bit panicked.

Being put on the spot and asked to communicate can feel like this. You often know what you think and intend to say, just like you know how to cross your arms. But when the setting changes—you're in a social situation and the pressure is on—you can feel confused, overwhelmed, threatened. Your fight-or-flight response kicks in—your heart pounds, your limbs shake, and you get hit by what I call "plumbing reversal": what normally is dry (your palms) becomes moist with sweat and what is normally moist (your mouth) goes dry. As you struggle to recover, you stammer, ramble, hesitate. You veer off on tangents. You stare at your feet or shrink down in your seat. You fidget. You overwhelm your audience with "ums" and "uhs."

You might even freeze up entirely. At the 2014 Consumer Electronics Show, Michael Bay, director of *Armageddon* and the Transformers franchise among other films, had trouble with a teleprompter as he was giving a presentation for a corporate sponsor. Forced to improvise, Bay was at a near-total loss for words, even though he was discussing a subject he knew well—his own movies. After fumbling for a couple of moments, it was all he could do to mutter a quick apology and walk offstage. One commentator wryly remarked that they hadn't "cringed like that since *Transformers 2.*"[3]

"Impromptu Speaking Isn't My Thing"

Bay later explained his performance that day by saying, "I guess live shows aren't my thing." Too often, people presume the ability to improvise on the fly is a matter of personality or inborn talent—some people have a knack for it, others don't. We tell ourselves we're just not gifted at thinking and speaking spontaneously. "I'm shy," we say, or "I'm a numbers person." Worse, some of us conclude we're not smart or good enough.

Sometimes a single disastrous episode can convince us for life that we're bad communicators. Irma, a librarian in her late sixties, yearned to deliver impromptu remarks at her beloved granddaughter's upcoming wedding, but sadly, the thought of standing up and speaking sent chills down her spine. When I asked about her fears, she told me they started decades earlier when she was in high school. She had responded to a question from her teacher, and he embarrassed her in front of her entire class by exclaiming, "That's the worst, most stupid answer I've ever had a student say in my class."

The experience not only prevented Irma from participating actively in meetings and other social encounters; it became a turning point in her life. She chose to become a research librarian precisely because she knew she'd rarely if ever have to engage in any stressful, unplanned communication on the job. Think about that for a moment. Irma put massive constraints on her life, simply because she feared a repeat of a single impromptu speaking debacle.

As extreme as that might sound, many of us do something similar. Past failures make us acutely aware of our inability to respond well, and we dread having to speak spontaneously again. On subsequent occasions, a vicious cycle can kick in: our nerves lead us to do even worse, which in turn makes us even more nervous, further inhibiting our ability to respond. At some point, the anxiety we feel becomes too much. With the "I can't do this" soundtrack playing in our heads, we shrink into the shadows, keeping our potentially great ideas and contributions to ourselves. We find seats in the back of the lecture hall or at the far end of the conference table. We disappear on Zoom calls by switching off our cameras and muting our mics.

Our professed and actual inability to communicate in impromptu settings can devastate our careers and lives. Years ago, when I worked for a small software start-up, a colleague of mine whom I'll call Chris had a great idea for how to position the company's Big Product. Since his idea was fairly radical, requiring a shift in our strategy, it came under considerable scrutiny. When others asked him to elaborate and posed hard but appropriate questions, Chris froze up. He seemed nervous and offered answers that were vague, rambling, and off-topic. Unimpressed, his boss and colleagues disregarded his opinions and downplayed his expertise. Eventually, the company let Chris go. Six months later, after new talent arrived, the company adopted Chris's very same ideas. The difference was that the new team could advocate for these ideas clearly and persuasively when put on the spot.

Thinking Fast and Talking Smart

I'm writing this book because there is hope for Irma, Chris, and anyone else out there challenged by spontaneous speaking. Consider the story of Archana, another student of mine who struggled when interacting with others. Having recently moved to the United States and changed professions, she felt unsure of herself and tended to avoid speaking up. "I judged myself harshly," she recalls. "I would get anxious and avoid speaking up in meetings at work." She realized that her reticence was putting her at a disadvantage, causing her to miss out on important career-building opportunities.

After working to learn and practice a set of proven tools and techniques, Archana found that she could relax more and be herself. Turning down the critical voices in her head, she felt more self-confident, which allowed her to speak out more and made future spontaneous speaking experiences easier. Before long, she was leading team meetings without feeling too much anxiety. When a colleague of hers passed away, she surprised herself by volunteering to stand up in public and share memories and kind words.

Some people are naturally more extroverted, uninhibited, quick-witted, or facile with words than others. But any deficits we might have in these areas need not define us nor determine our destiny. What most shapes how we communicate on the fly isn't something innate or deeply established in us but rather how we approach this challenging task.

Most of us conceive of spontaneous social interaction in ways that box us in and thwart us. Building up these interactions in our minds, we freak ourselves out, preventing ourselves from operating well in the moment. In other words, we get in our own way. By lowering the pressure we put on ourselves and by practicing some key skills, we can become better, more competent communicators in any kind of unplanned, high-stakes conversation. We can even come alive in these situations and *enjoy* them. We can all learn to, as I call it, think faster and talk smarter.

No matter how affable, sociable, and facile with words we perceive ourselves to be, we can all become more comfortable and confident in the moment by employing the Think Faster, Talk Smarter method you will find outlined in this book, as well as the context-specific structures I've provided.

This method has six steps:

First, we must acknowledge what we already know—that communication in general and impromptu speaking in particular are nerve-racking. We must create a personalized anxiety management plan to help address our jitters.

Second, we must reflect on our approach to communication and how we judge ourselves and others, seeing these situations as opportunities for connection and collaboration.

Third, we must give ourselves permission to adopt new mindsets, take risks, and reenvision mistakes as missed takes.

Fourth, we must listen deeply to what others are saying (and perhaps not saying) while also tuning in to our own internal voice and intuition.

Fifth, we must leverage story structure to make our ideas more intelligible, sharper, and more compelling than they might otherwise have been.

And sixth, we must focus audiences as much as possible on the essence of what we're saying, cultivating precision, relevance, accessibility, and concision.

We can perform some of the work that these six steps require in the moment as we're speaking by adopting a range of helpful tactics. But more fundamentally, these six steps represent skills that we must cultivate over time as we prepare for spontaneous encounters we think we're likely to have. Many people presume that speaking well when put on the spot requires natural talent—quick-wittedness or the gift of gab. While some of us certainly possess these talents, the real secret to spontaneous speaking is *practice* and *preparation*. All of us can become strong speakers in the moment if we put in the time, learning to break old habits and exercise more deliberate choices. Paradoxically, we have to prepare in advance to do well in spontaneous situations, working hard on skills that we know will free us up to bring out our ideas and personalities to the fullest.

As when learning any new skill, it helps to reduce the pressure you put on yourself. Remember that becoming a strong communicator when put on the spot takes time. You don't have to stress yourself out trying to do it all at once. Moreover, the very fact that you're focusing on improving yourself in this way is already worth celebrating. Most people either don't think about spontaneous speaking, or if they do, they aren't courageous enough to do anything about it. You *are* aware and brave, as evidenced by the fact that you picked up this book in the first place.

Becoming adept at spontaneous communication takes patience, commitment, and grace, but as the people I coach and teach have found, the impact can be life-changing.

Life Isn't a TED Talk

One of the most persistent and unhelpful myths we harbor about spontaneous communication is the notion that the best, most compelling communicators express themselves perfectly. Just look at how polished those successful TED Talk presenters are, even though they're speaking casually, without notes. Or look at leaders like Apple's Steve Jobs or former first lady Michelle Obama, who were or are famously charismatic and compelling when they appear before large audiences.

In truth, TED Talks are heavily scripted and sometimes even edited. Leaders like Jobs and Obama spend months practicing and refining their presentations. We often confuse these planned, perfected communications with what we encounter more frequently in our lives: spontaneous, off-the-cuff remarks. We evaluate how we do in these everyday situations using standards we apply to rehearsed talks. That's a mistake. Rather than aiming for perfection, as we might do in our presentations, we should instead embrace *imperfection* and focus on how we might best engage in the moment. By training ourselves to quiet down our critical evaluation, we can lower our stress levels and better accomplish our communication goals.

In truth, striving to get our communication "right" only increases the odds that we'll communicate poorly. If we try to memorize our way to success or fixate on one way of speaking, we'll focus so much on trying to remember what we've worked on that we'll likely freeze up in the moment and fail to tune in to what's happening around us. We'll lose out on the chance to adapt and respond authentically in the moment. We'll distance ourselves from what we really must do to think faster and talk smarter: be ourselves, stay present, and connect with our audience.

A classical musician performing a Chopin étude in public memorizes every last note in advance in hopes of achieving perfection. But speaking extemporaneously is more like jazz. It's about improvising, trying to get and stay in the groove with others around us. To be good improvisers and spontaneous communicators, we must set aside much of what we think we know about communication and master a new set of skills. We must cue in quickly and accurately to our environment. We must gauge our audience's needs. We must adapt what we're saying to those needs. And we must manage our fears so they don't limit us.

This is not to say that planning and rehearsing have no place in everyday communication. They do. But many of us already have developed and honed these skills—perhaps too much. Now we must balance ourselves out by working on our spontaneous speaking, too. We must learn new approaches and tools that allow us to take our tried-and-true communication habits and practices and turn them into *choices* we make as needed in the moment.

The Virtues of the Letter A

Remember Irma, who became a librarian because of unpleasant feedback she received? I had a very different experience while growing up. You might have noticed from perusing this book's cover that my last name begins with *Ab*. This mundane fact shaped my life in ways that help account for the book you hold in your hands. Because teachers and other authority figures tend to call on people in alphabetical order by last name, I've almost always been called on first. In fact, I can only think of two times throughout my childhood and on into adulthood when I *wasn't* called on first (the other last names were Abbott and Abbey, in case you're wondering).

Since I always went first, I never had any other examples to draw on when formulating answers, and I often had little time to prepare. Even in elementary school, I was the kid who always had to respond spontaneously. At first, doing so felt awkward. But then I started to get used to it. I let myself open up a little, take chances, experiment, make jokes. Other kids seemed grateful to hear me share my ideas before the teacher called on them.

This positive reinforcement spurred me to take more risks, be less nervous, and embrace opportunities when they arose. By high school, people knew me as an extrovert who was always willing to talk and go first. Some even found me witty, entertaining, or charming. Now, am I innately witty, entertaining, or charming? Heck no—just ask my children. I simply had a lot of experience improvising in everyday social situations, and my constant practice made spontaneous communication feel second nature.

I want *you* to feel as comfortable and confident in impromptu speaking situations as I have become. And you needn't change your last name to do it.

From Stanford with Love

During the early 2010s, professors at Stanford's Graduate School of Business, where I teach, noticed an interesting trend. Many of my colleagues test our students' knowledge by cold-calling on them in front of dozens or hundreds of their peers. We would assign case studies as homework and then pick on one or more students in class, often asking them enough questions to make Socrates proud.

Our students were bright, articulate, and motivated. They could craft and deliver a formal speech with the best of them. Many of them had given speeches as valedictorians or as part of their previous work experience. Yet, these students struggled with in-class cold calls. Many would come to class highly anxious or sit out class on days they anticipated being called upon. They tended to freeze up when put on the spot. Although students knew the answers, they struggled to quickly come up with sharp, incisive responses.

As the "communication guy" on campus who cotaught classes at Stanford's Graduate School of Business and Continuing Studies program, I was asked to design a new learning experience to help with spontaneous social interactions in class, one that would complement our existing course offerings on formal communication. I set to work, reading everything I could that related to spontaneous communication. I consulted academic journals in fields like communication, psychology, evolutionary biology, sociology, and education. I also reviewed improvisational comedy textbooks and studied examples of spontaneous communication in politics, business, medicine, and other domains. Most importantly, I called upon what I'd learned from colleagues around the Stanford campus, many of whom you'll meet in this book.

Integrating all of this material as well as experiences I'd had coteaching the Stanford Continuing Studies Improvisationally Speaking class with lecturer Adam Tobin, I created a workshop with the provocative yet grammatically incorrect title of "Think Fast, Talk Smart: Effective Speaking in Spontaneous and Stressful Situations." To my surprise and delight, this workshop has become something of a tradition at our business school. Most Stanford MBAs learn how to think fast and talk smart before they graduate. I have presented this material online (through videos and a podcast) and at companies, nonprofits, and government groups so that more people can think fast and talk smart.

The response has been amazing. Students report liking their classes more because they no longer fear the dreaded cold call. Others who found me online share how my techniques have helped them ace interviews, secure funding, pass oral exams, win over new customers, impress bosses, and even get engaged. Corporate clients report that the tools I teach lead to better communication, stronger relationships, more enjoyable workplace experiences, and ultimately, better business results.

What if *you* could become more comfortable and confident with spontaneous communication? What if getting singled out to speak didn't feel like a trial or tribulation but rather a chance to engage, learn, connect, and perhaps even have fun? What if you could lose all those self-doubts, sweaty palms, and stilted pauses and communicate in ways that are more logical, concise, and compelling? What if you could rise to the occasion, thinking fast and talking smart when the spotlight falls on you?

Now you can. *Think Faster, Talk Smarter* is a concise, practical methodology you can use to finally feel good about communicating on the fly. Part I shares a powerful, six-part method for understanding the obstacles that so often interfere with impromptu speaking. I'll show you how to identify the key challenges that ratchet up the pressure in spontaneous communication situations. Although you may not have thought about all of these challenges, they cropped up consistently in my work with academics, entrepreneurs, and other thought leaders. You'll learn how to manage your anxieties (chapter 1: Calm), prevent perfectionism from holding you back (chapter 2: Unlock), and avoid a closed or resistant mindset (chapter 3: Redefine). Next, I'll impart specific tools and tactics you can use to excel. You'll learn how to listen actively to your audience to understand what is really needed in the situation (chapter 4: Listen), structure content on the fly (chapter 5: Structure), and streamline your ideas so they're focused and compelling (chapter 6: Focus).

Part II addresses some of the most common contexts in which we're called to express ourselves in the moment. I'll explore specific techniques for navigating common communication challenges, such as giving feedback effectively and shining in interview situations. I'll describe strategies I have used when preparing entrepreneurs to effectively pitch ideas and opportunities to others; to engage in successful small talk; to give impromptu toasts, tributes, and introductions that audiences will love; and even to apologize in ways that resonate powerfully. I have included a summary of these structures in the first appendix.

Finally, I provide a QR code in the second appendix that will take you to a dedicated *Think Faster, Talk Smarter* website that I will update often with new materials and videos discussing and demonstrating concepts from the book and offering new ones.

If you have come to this book to prepare for a specific speaking opportunity, you may feel tempted to jump straight to part II or appendices of the book, and that's okay. Just know that more fundamental strategies for transforming your communication abilities await you in part I when you're ready.

All along, I'll challenge conventional wisdom, providing counter-intuitive techniques to help us navigate all kinds of tricky, in-the-moment communications tasks. To make the material more memorable, I'll highlight specific tactics to try out (I label these "Try It") and exercises that allow us to practice key techniques in more depth ("Drill It"). As I'll suggest, we can use these techniques to help us recover from faux pas, deescalate volatile situations, receive and deliver bad news more gracefully, flirt more easily with that attractive someone, shine in cocktail parties, and in general respond in ways that are more affable, charming, and effective.

Stepping Up in the Moment

Of course, I can't promise that you'll perform perfectly in any specific situation just by learning these techniques. But to be honest, I wouldn't want you to perform perfectly every time. Spontaneous situations are by definition . . . spontaneous. Those who do best are flexible, agile, and creative in applying the tools and techniques I discuss. They can adjust their communication to suit the room and the mood. Still, having a methodology in your back pocket as you go through life can make a huge difference. It helps you feel more comfortable and confident in approaching any in-the-moment speaking situation, giving you a basis for navigating situations that might otherwise seem overwhelming.

Mastering spontaneous communication is like learning a sport. First you absorb the foundational principles, and then you apply them in practice situations. You might not hit a home run during the big game or score the winning point, but at least you'll take substantive steps toward your goal and feel good about how you did.

The key is to trust your training, give yourself permission to take risks, challenge what already feels comfortable, and experiment. Don't abandon everything you already know. Just explore and incorporate an alternate approach, familiarizing yourself with an area of communication that is often overlooked. Use this book as a guide for ongoing practice. Turn to it before your next big conference, meeting, wedding, travel opportunity, media appearance—any situation in which you anticipate a need to communicate in the moment and want to shine. By adding tools and techniques to your communication repertoire, you'll be better able to speak up effectively no matter what comes your way.

It's funny—we humans are ill-equipped to show up for some of the most meaningful moments in our life. These moments catch us by surprise, short-circuiting our intelligence and leaving us to project just a fraction of our true personalities. We can do something about this. We can train ourselves to think and speak on our feet, reacting in ways that come across as coherent, compelling, and unmistakably genuine. We can learn to be more of who we really are in the moment and convey more of what we really think. So, let's get started. By understanding and practicing the following six steps, you, too, can start to think faster and talk smarter.

PART I

The Think Faster, Talk Smarter Methodology—
Six Steps to Better Spontaneous Speaking

CALM · UNLOCK · REDEFINE · LISTEN · STRUCTURE · FOCUS

Chapter 1: Calm

TAME THE ANXIETY BEAST

With a bit of effort, we can manage our spontaneous
speaking anxiety so that it doesn't manage us.

Peeling onions almost always makes me cry, but there was a time long ago when an onion caused a very different emotional response—sheer panic! I was interviewing for a job as employee number ninety-nine at an up-and-coming software company. I made it through several rounds, and the last step was to sit for an interview with the CEO, who prided himself on personally meeting everyone before they were hired.

When I arrived at the appointed time, I found the Big Boss already waiting for me. That threw me a little—in my experience, senior executives were so busy that they usually arrived late. But I was about to field another, more substantive curveball. Just a minute or two into our conversation, the CEO posed a question I never could have anticipated (it turned out he was famous for asking open-ended questions to test how people would respond under pressure). "If you were an onion," he said, "and I peeled back the first three layers, what would I find?"

Um . . . *okay.* I was expecting to talk about topics such as my educational credentials, my past experience, my goals, and the reasons I believed I was a good fit for the company. Why was he asking me about onions?

Despite all the practice I had with spontaneous speaking growing up, I now experienced the kind of fight-or-flight response most of us struggle with in such situations. My shoulders tensed. My throat went

17

dry. My brain was overloaded. I felt jittery and hot. I really wanted to ace this interview, but my nerves were getting the better of me. I had no idea what to say.

Speaking Up without Freaking Out

To improve at spontaneous communication, or frankly any kind of communication, we must first learn to manage the intense anxiety that can arise. As I've suggested, an attack of nerves can overpower us, consuming our attention, energy, and ability to execute.[1] We can even become caught in what we might call an *anxiety spiral.* Our anxiety leads us to fault ourselves and lose confidence—we feel alone, disempowered, marginalized. That produces still more anxiety.[2] At the extreme, this spiral can cause us to choke when put on the spot. Our anxiety overwhelms our ability to cope with it.[3]

The good news is that we can adopt techniques to reduce our anxiety, becoming more comfortable communicating ideas in any situation without our anxiety kicking into high gear. We can also become more compelling to others.

The goal isn't to eradicate anxiety but rather to prevent it from hampering us. Some situations will always freak us out. And that's actually okay—a bit of anxiety is a good thing. Too much stress impedes us from completing tasks successfully, but experiments have suggested that a certain amount of it helps to motivate us.[4] When we feel moderately stressed or fearful, our bodies become energized and primed for action, our minds become more alert and focused, and we become more attuned to others around us. Research with rats suggests that acute stress can improve memory by causing new nerve cells to form in the brain.[5]

In my experience, the best way to tame the speaking anxiety beast is to take a two-pronged approach. First, tackle the *symptoms* of anxiety that pop up in the moment. Second, address anxiety's underlying *sources.* In this chapter, we'll focus primarily on symptoms, while later in the book we'll discuss some of anxiety's sources. When it comes to symptoms, some simple techniques can help. Mobilizing these techniques in the moment and in advance of anticipated spontaneous speaking situations, we can feel far more comfortable and confident, and we can respond more effectively. The next time we're in a job interview or some other spontaneous speaking situation and we're surprised with a proverbial peeling-back-the-onion question, we'll be in a far better position to handle it.

Know Your ABCs

I've noted in passing many of the symptoms people often feel when anxious. It turns out we can group these into a few simple categories— what we can call the ABCs of speaking anxiety.[6]

When others put us on the spot, we experience *affective* symptoms, those relating to our mood or how we feel. People under the spotlight often feel stressed, pressured, or lacking in agency. They feel vulnerable, overwhelmed, and frightened.

We also experience symptoms that are *behavioral* or physiological in nature. We sweat. Tremble. Stutter. Our heart races. Our voice shakes. Our breathing becomes shallow. Our speech becomes faster, more jittery. Our faces become flushed. Our mouths go dry.

A third and final category of symptoms are *cognitive*. We become flustered, blanking out or forgetting what we want or need to say. We fixate on our awareness of others watching us and can't focus on our audiences and their needs. We experience negative thoughts or self-talk, a little voice in our heads that tells us we're not prepared, we're likely to fail, others are better than us, and so on.

Mindfulness Matters

Let's explore how we might tackle these symptoms, starting with the affective ones. A powerful way to address unhelpful or negative feelings that arise in the moment is to practice mindfulness.[7] Notice and acknowledge the unpleasant feelings, don't ignore or deny them, and don't berate yourself for experiencing them. As you're experiencing these feelings, affirm their inability to define you as a person. As Stanford professor S. Christian Wheeler relates, "There's me and then there's this anxious feeling that is going on in my body. That amount of psychological distance allows you to observe it without becoming attached to it."[8]

● ● ● TRY IT ● ● ●

The next time you feel a negative emotion like anxiety, remind yourself that you and the emotion are not the same thing. Imagine you were someone else observing you experiencing the emotion.

Greet your feelings head-on, reminding yourself that it's normal and natural to feel anxious and that most people in your situation would, too. "Right now, I'm nervous," you might tell yourself. "I'm nervous because this is high-stakes for me. My reputation is on the line. This reaction makes sense and is normal." Permitting yourself to notice and identify how your mind and body are behaving can help you to regain a sense of agency or control when you would otherwise feel lost and distracted. By affirming that your negative feelings are normal and natural, you prevent the emotion from sweeping you away. You give yourself just a bit of space to break free and help yourself—by taking a deep breath, perhaps, or by imagining how you might respond to what someone next to you just said.

As you become aware of your feelings, you can go further and reframe them in more positive ways that energize rather than stymie you. People who become anxious before speaking often think they must try to calm themselves. Some make use of alcohol or other substances; others focus on visualizations like the famous *Brady Bunch* advice to imagine your audience "sitting in their underwear"[9] These measures often do more harm than good because they can leave you mentally fuzzy or distracted. As my friend Professor Alison Wood Brooks suggests, a better strategy might be to reframe anxiety as excitement. In a series of experiments, she showed that people who told themselves that they were excited (by stating "I am excited" out loud) before public speaking improved how they did. They also came to feel more excited and to see their speaking as an opportunity rather than a threat (more on this later).[10]

It turns out that anxiety affects your body in much the same way as excitement does. Both put us in a state of "very high alertness." Like mindfulness, reframing anxiety as something you are excited about affords us a sense of agency. We can't control our basic physiological response to the perceived threat posed by speaking, but we can control how we understand and label it. Feeling that sense of control shifts our experience of speaking and helps us to do better at it.

Slow Down, Cool Down, and Dampen Up

To address behavioral symptoms, one tried-and-true method is to focus on your breathing. Take some deep, long belly breaths, the kind you would do if you were practicing yoga or tai chi. Really fill your lower abdomen. As you'll find, breathing in this way allows you to feel calmer and slows your heart rate as well as the pace of your speech.

As you breathe, focus on the relative length of inhalations and exhalations. I was privileged to have the neuroscientist Andrew Huberman appear on my *Think Fast, Talk Smart: The Podcast*. As he observed, the magic of deep breathing when it comes to alleviating anxiety is in the exhalation. When you exhale, you're reducing carbon dioxide in your lungs, which in turn calms your nervous system. A good rule of thumb—or should I say, rule of lung—is to make exhalations twice as long as inhalations. Count to three as you inhale, and exhale over a count of six. Studies show that deep breathing of this sort starts to calm your nervous system in a matter of seconds.[11] Run through this pattern of breathing just two or three times and your heart rate will begin to slow.

You'll find that the rate at which you speak will slow as well. Speaking is all about breath and breath control. The faster you breathe, the faster you speak. Slow your breathing, and your speech also will naturally slow.

If you're a fast talker, you might find that deep breathing alone doesn't slow you down. In that case, try slowing your movements—your hand motions, the nodding of your head, the twisting of your torso, and so on. We tend to synchronize our speech with our gestures. Fast talkers gesture quickly, using swift, jerky motions. Slow down our movements, and our speech will slow as well.

As part of the fight-or-flight response, our bodies release adrenaline, a hormone that prompts us to move away from a threat and toward safety. Adrenaline causes our heart rate to rise and our muscles to tighten and become shaky. Turning our bodies to address a different side of the room or making small hand gestures can help to dissipate shakiness by fulfilling our need to move.[12] If you're giving an impromptu toast at a wedding, try walking slowly from one side to the next as you speak (ever notice that attorneys on TV always seem to do that when handling questions from the judge or addressing the jury?). You don't want to distract people by pacing too much, but taking a few steps in one direction as you shift between points can ease any shakiness you may feel.

What can you do about the blushing and perspiration unleashed when you're put on the spot? Quite a lot. When you're under stress, your core body temperature rises. Your heart beats more quickly, your muscles tense, your blood vessels constrict, and your blood pressure and body temperature rise. All of this causes you to sweat and blush, just as it does when exercising.

You can counteract these effects by cooling your body. Focus here on your hands. Just like your forehead or the back of your neck, your hands serve to regulate your body temperature. Have you ever warmed up on a cold morning by holding a warm cup of coffee or tea? That's your built-in thermoregulator in action. At moments when you're put on the spot or you think you're about to be, try holding something cold in your hand, like a bottle or glass of water. I do it all the time in speaking situations when I'm anxious (yes, I sometimes get anxious, too). It really helps.

Finally, let's do something about that annoying dry mouth that might arise as you try to communicate. When you become nervous, your salivary glands shut down. Reactivate them by sipping warm water, sucking on a lozenge, or chewing gum. It's best not to do this in the moment, since stuffing up your mouth can make speaking difficult. But if you're entering a situation where you suspect you might be called upon to communicate, taking a moment to prepare in advance by reactivating your salivary glands is a good move.

Tame Your Brain

Let's say I'm hosting an important Zoom call with two dozen colleagues and customers, and the technology fails, cutting off my colleague who was supposed to be presenting for the next fifteen minutes. Someone has to fill in the empty space—that would be me, the team leader. But as my body goes into fight-or-flight, I'm hearing these dark little voices in my head: "I don't know what to say. Everybody's judging me. I'm going to get fired over this."

I can banish that nasty little voice and take back control by repeating a more positive mantra in my head. Professional golfers often do this, repeating a word like "calm" or "poise" to tamp down negative self-talk. We can also adopt mantras that remind us of our deeper purposes. In a spontaneous communication situation, you might tell yourself something like:

- "I have value to add."
- "I've improvised my way out of tough spots before—I've got this."
- "It's not about me—my content is compelling."

Repeating a mantra can allow us to redirect our thoughts, unchaining us from the doom loop running through our minds.[13]

If you blank out, try going back to go forward. Recall what was just said and repeat it. Doing this can give yourself a moment to get yourself back on track. Many people deploy a similar tactic when they lose their keys: they go back in their minds to every place they might have been, which in turn might jog their memory of where they left them.

You might think that repeating what you just said is a no-no, as it will bore or distract your audience. If you do it fifty times in a three-minute period, that might be true. But in general, repetition is a good thing. When you repeat a point a few times, you highlight it for your audiences and help them remember it. Saying something in different ways can help ideas become more comprehensible and noteworthy. Repetition is okay. You see? I just did it—I repeated the same idea three times. That wasn't so bad, was it?

You can also buy yourself time by posing generic questions that might make sense given the context. I'll let you in on a secret. When I teach, I sometimes lose my train of thought. I teach so many classes that I can't remember if I've made a certain point in this class or the other one. This momentary confusion can freak me out, and I feel compelled to respond immediately lest I look foolish. Typically, I'll pause and say, "Before we move on, I'd like you to take a moment to think about how you might apply what we've just discussed to your life."

Now, I'm fortunate. Because I teach communication, students can in fact apply much of what I talk about right away. But I'll bet you could quickly come up with a generic question that you could ask, one that would allow you to take a deep breath and reflect on where you want to go next.

In a Zoom call, for instance, you might ask something like, "Can you think of ways you can share this information with your teammates?" Or when leading a meeting, you could say, "Let's pause for a moment and just think about how what we've been discussing fits into our overall objectives."

A simple question gets people thinking and lets you off the hook as the center of attention for a moment so that you can regain your composure. If you know that you'll be attending an event (a team lunch, conference, or wedding) in which you might be asked to speak spontaneously, you might think of one of these questions in advance and keep it handy just in case.

● ● ● TRY IT ● ● ●

The next time you enter a situation where you think you might have to speak spontaneously, come prepared with a question to ask your audience if you become flustered.

If the mere thought of blanking out arouses fear in the moment, having these tools handy can give you an extra bit of comfort and security. You might also try rationalizing before you get into a likely spontaneous speaking situation. Ask yourself what the chances are that you really will blank out. Most people thinking rationally might put the odds that the situation wouldn't go well at 20 or 25 percent. But that means you'll have a 75 or 80 percent chance that it will. I'll take those odds.

Further, ask yourself: If I do blank out, what's the worst that can happen? Many of us would say something like, "I'll be embarrassed," or "It will be awkward," or "I might not see the career growth I'm looking for," or "People might not want to talk to me." We can make a long list of terrible consequences. But we should put our fears into perspective and realize that these consequences probably won't come to pass. People are often so consumed with their own anxieties and the impression they are leaving that they aren't paying that much attention to us. This phenomenon is so well known that psychologists have a name for it: the *spotlight effect*.[14] Most likely, we are dramatically overestimating any negative impressions that others might have of us on account of our speaking.

The rationalization process takes the edge off anxiety, offering us just a bit of agency. You can also reduce the odds of blanking out by structuring what you say in the moment. Structure provides you with a map, and it's much harder to get lost and blank out if you have one. You might presume that you can only structure your remarks well by planning them out in advance, but that's not true. As we'll see in chapter 5, you can do it very effectively in the moment as well.

Um ... Uh ... Like ... You Know

In addressing cognitive symptoms, we must do something about those annoying filler words that pop out of our mouths when we are working out what we want to say. I'm not saying you need to banish these words entirely; some use of filler words is natural and normal, so much so that scriptwriters actually write them into dialogues in movies, television, and plays. The issue is that *excessive* use of filler words—common culprits such as "um," "uh," and "like"—can become distracting, acting as a kind of verbal graffiti. Fortunately, there is a technique you can deploy that can stop these types of words from ever appearing. Once again it has to do with breathing.

Take a deep breath in. As you exhale, I'd like you to say, "Um." Can you do that? Great. Now I'd like you to say "um" while inhaling. You can't do it, can you? It's nearly impossible to say anything while inhaling. Speaking is an exit-only event. You must push air out to do it. And this fact holds the key to ridding us of those filler words that occur between sentences and phrases.

The trick is this: when you speak, work to articulate your sentences and phrases so that you're completely out of breath at the end of the sentence or phrase. Try it a few times—it's not hard, and you don't have to use long sentences or phrases to do it. Just time your exhalation to coincide with the completion of a sentence or phrase. I envision a gymnast sticking their landing. If you synch your speaking with your breathing in this way, you'll have to inhale upon finishing a sentence or phrase. That will make it more difficult for you to utter a filler word.

This technique also helps by building a short pause into your speech. As communicators, we often presume that we must fill all of the airtime, and that any empty space is awkward. Not true! Sprinkling in pauses allows your audience to catch up and reflect on what you just said.

● ● ● TRY IT ● ● ●

To practice synching sentences and phrases with your breath, I recommend talking through a series of sentences. At the end of each one, you want to "land" by coming down in tone and being out of breath. Think of the steps required to perform a common, everyday action. If you talk through an activity you know well, you don't have to think about what you're saying as much, and you can focus on the ending of the sentences. I like to talk through the process of making a peanut butter and jelly sandwich: "First, you take out two pieces of bread." "Then, you spread peanut butter on one slice, but not too much." "Then, you spread jelly on the other slice, but not too much." "Then you put the slices together." "The jelly side of one piece should face the peanut butter side of the other." "Slice the sandwich in half and enjoy." When you reach each of the underlined words, look to land your phrase and ensure that you are out of breath. To take your practice further, you might try working with speaking preparation tools such as Poised. com, Orai, and LikeSo, which provide valuable feedback on your use of filler words.

The chart below summarizes the various techniques you can employ to help manage your spontaneous speaking anxiety.

Techniques for Minding Your Anxiety Symptom ABCs

Technique	Description	Commentary
Practice Mindfulness	Acknowledge your feelings and sit with them.	These feelings are perfectly rational and normal.
Breathe	Inhale deeply, filling your lower abdomen as you breathe deliberately.	Deep or yoga-like breaths dispel anxiety. Exhale twice as long as your inhale.
Slow Your Movements	Slow your hand gestures and other movements.	Your speech often keeps pace with your bodily movements. Slow them down and watch your speech calm as well.
Cool Your Body	Hold a cool bottle of water or other cold object in your hands.	By cooling yourself down, you blush and perspire less.
Salivate	Chew on some gum or enjoy a lozenge.	Chewing reactivates your salivary glands.
Positive Self-Talk	Recite a positive mantra in your head.	This will quiet your inner critic and positively redirect your thoughts.
Rewind and Question to Progress	Repeat yourself and ask questions.	Avoid repeating too often, but to jog your memory repeat what you just said or pose some questions to your audience.

Technique	Description	Commentary
Get Rational	Tell yourself the "worst" that could happen if you screw this up. (Hint: even the worst isn't that bad).	People are mostly focused on themselves and not you. Remember that and rationality will prevail.
Inhale to Reduce Fillers	Land phrases so you need to inhale.	Watch all the filler words ("like," "okay") disappear.

● ● ● TRY IT ● ● ●

Create a spontaneous speaking tool kit, outfitted with all you need to manage your anxiety in the moment. Include, for instance, a cold bottle of water, a lozenge, and a note card with an affirmation written on it. Given the tips provided in this chapter, what else might you add to this kit to customize it just for you? Keep this kit handy in your phone, wallet, or purse so that you can access it just before the next event when you anticipate having to speak spontaneously.

AMP Yourself Up

To succeed in tackling symptoms of anxiety, we must also work to make these interventions stick. Take a few moments to ponder the techniques I've shared. Which of these seem most interesting, natural, or helpful? Have you tried any of them already? Have you used other anxiety-calming techniques in different areas of your life (for instance, when you're playing a sport or flirting) that might help you with your speaking fears?

Once you've reviewed the techniques, gather together your favorites and form them into what I call a personalized Anxiety Management Plan (AMP). By contributing to your sense of agency and focus, your AMP can help excite or amp you up about speaking. Pick a handful of techniques (between three to five of them) that you believe will work for you and that address specific anxiety symptoms that bedevil you the most. (You may also want to incorporate techniques for addressing the underlying sources of speaking anxiety. I'll describe some of those later in the book.) Then think of an acronym that might help you remember them in the moment. Here are a couple of examples:

Sample Anxiety Management Plans

BOOM

Be present oriented: Focus on what is happening in the moment rather than worry about potential negative future consequences.
Observe your movements: Slow your gestures to moderate your speaking pace.
Oxygenate: Exhale twice as long as you inhale.
Mantra: Speak a word or phrase that can help you calm down and focus.

ARC

Acknowledge that anxiety is normal: Recognize you're not the only one.
Rationalize: Remind yourself that even if you totally flop, it's not the end of the world.
Cool yourself down: Hold something cold in your hand to keep your body temperature low.

I ask all of my students and consulting clients to create an AMP. They routinely thank me, writing years later to report that they still are deploying these techniques. As they attest, finding and deploying the right AMP supercharges their confidence when they speak in high-stakes, spontaneous situations. Small changes sustained over time really do make a big difference.

One woman I work with, Stephanie, took over as CEO of her family business when she was in her late twenties. In this role, she had to connect with her seventy-five employees of diverse backgrounds and project an authoritative persona. Her task became even more difficult when COVID struck and disrupted the business. Employees who in some cases were decades older felt anxious and looked to her for leadership. As she made controversial decisions to stabilize the business, they grilled her about changes they would experience.

Stephanie found daily communication extraordinarily stressful—even more so because she wasn't a native speaker of English. She became self-conscious and would reveal her anxiety by stumbling over words and adopting a guarded, humorless demeanor. Her anxiety became so intense that she had difficulty sleeping and focusing on day-to-day tasks. She even thought about stepping down as CEO.

To help Stephanie, we developed an AMP that steered her away from fixating on future goals. Over time, she wound up deepening and modifying her AMP, taking it in a direction that was all her own. When I checked in on her in the spring of 2022, her AMP had come to revolve around three phrases meaningful to her: Heart, Speech, and Mind, or HSM. "Heart" referred to why she was speaking: she found that she was less anxious if she reminded herself of her intention to be of service to her audience and to concentrate on them and their needs, not herself. "Speech" focused her on what she needed to do technically to connect with her audience. Knowing that she tended to speed up and stumble over her words when nervous, she made a point of gesturing more slowly and asking questions to force herself to pause. "Mind" was a cue to remind herself that the actual likelihood of blanking out and messing up was far lower than she feared.

Stephanie is continuing to work on her anxiety, but thanks to her ongoing efforts with her AMP and the techniques described in this chapter, her anxiety has become more manageable. She leads others more effectively and enjoys her job more. In fact, she has begun to coach others to become more confident in their communication.

An AMP is not a quick fix but rather an ongoing experiment, with each technique amounting to a hypothesis. Once you've generated your AMP, test it out in real-life situations. Rehearse your AMP to yourself before you go into your next work meeting or dinner party. Try the techniques in the moment. Did they help? If not, try swapping in other techniques (and don't forget to update the acronym).

There is no quick and easy solution for speaking anxiety. What we can do is engage in a more gradual process of managing this emotion so that it does not interfere with our communication goals.

Discovering YOU

Being comfortable thinking on your feet is important for formal speeches and presentations; it holds special relevance when you're called to speak spontaneously. As we'll see in the next chapter, managing anxiety ultimately frees you to behave more naturally and authentically when put on the spot. You become bolder, nimbler, more playful, and looser. You're able to tune in better to your audience's needs and react appropriately. You're able to take more *joy* in communicating. All of this allows you to become more compelling as a speaker—to speak up without freaking out.

When that CEO asked me what he'd find if I were an onion and he peeled back my first three layers, I went into fight-or-flight. But I didn't let my nerves get the better of me. Instead, I initiated part of my AMP—I took a deep breath and repeated my mantra, "I have value to offer." Almost immediately, I was able to recover and free myself up to improvise.

I wound up focusing on the onion itself and drawing inspiration for the rest of my answer from there. "Onions make me cry," I said. "Whenever I cut them, I tear up. I don't know, maybe it's just me—I cry easily. In fact, I often look to surround myself with people who are willing to cry and show how they feel."

I went on to talk about how in my previous job I hired people who were passionate and willing to share their emotions. This openness and energy made my team cohesive and supportive. While we sometimes disagreed with one another, we each knew where we stood and respected our colleagues and their perspectives. Conveying this example to the CEO led to a deeper discussion about empathy, trust, and psychological safety, their importance in my life, and my desire to bring them to the role for which I was interviewing.

Committing to focusing on the onion and seeing where it led me was an important decision I took in the moment, and one that I might not have had the courage and clarity to make had I been consumed with anxiety. As I answered, I noticed that the CEO was smiling—he hadn't expected an answer like this. Most candidates had probably said something like, "If you peeled back the onion, you'd learn that I'm diligent," or "You'd learn that I'm honest." In my case, he got a creative, unusual, and poignant answer that conveyed something unique about me. I wound up getting the job and having an amazing time at the company. I had no inkling of it then, but that job would alter the trajectory of my career.

While I'm sure many factors contributed to the company's decision to hire me, it didn't hurt that I had been able to react well after the CEO had put me on the spot. You can let your personality shine in these kinds of situations, too. Managing your anxiety so that it doesn't manage you is the essential first step.

● ● ● DRILL IT ● ● ●

1. Take the AMP you created and deploy it in your next spontaneous speaking situation. Reflect on how it went, what worked, and what didn't. What's one thing you would change to make it better for the next time?

2. The next time you experience a strong positive or negative emotion, take a moment to acknowledge and accept it. How does it feel? Reflect on why the emotion might be coming up for you. Does it make sense given the circumstances you are in? If someone else were to share that they were experiencing this emotion, could you help them understand why it was appropriate and reasonable?

3. Challenge yourself to perform five minutes of deep breathing each day for a week. During this time, go to a quiet
   place and focus on your breath. Make sure that your exhalations are twice as long as your inhalations. Notice how
   you feel at the end of each session.

Chapter 2: Unlock

MAXIMIZE MEDIOCRITY

When it comes to spontaneous speaking,
good enough is great.

A nxiety is a pretty heavy topic. So, let's relax a little and play a game called Shout the Wrong Name.[1] Not familiar with it? You're in for a treat.

I first fell in love with this game when I saw Adam Tobin, my friend and improv mentor, demonstrate and debrief it in the class we coteach called Improvisationally Speaking. The game is simple. If you're sitting at your desk or in a nice, cushy chair, please stand and meander around the room. Just wander anywhere, changing direction periodically. Or, you could do this outside—a little fresh air never hurt anyone.

As you walk, point to a random object and call out its name. Except I'd like you to call out the *wrong* name. If you point to a houseplant, call it "horse," "pink," "regardless," "cheeseburger," or "gee whiz"— anything *except* "houseplant." Once you've done this, point to another object and blurt out its wrong name, whatever comes to mind. If it's the same name you gave to the houseplant, that's okay.

Keep pointing to objects as quickly as you can and naming them out loud incorrectly, using whatever words pop into your brain. Do this for, say, fifteen or twenty seconds and then stop.

How did you do? Was it easy to come up with wrong names? This game seems simple, but if you are like most people, you actually found it quite challenging.

When students and other audience members play this game, they tend to move slowly and cautiously around the room pointing but not speaking. Their faces grow pensive, as if they were trying to reduce a polynomial to its most basic form. They avoid eye contact with me or others. Afterward, they talk about how hard they found this task. "I felt stupid," they say. "I'm no good at this." They even say, "You're mean for making me feel foolish."

As psychologists have documented, our brains more easily process stimuli that conform to expected patterns than they do stimuli that are unexpected. For example, if you ask people to read the names of colors (purple, blue, orange), they find it easier when those names are written in the same color ink as the word. If you see "purple" written in orange ink, your brain will do a double take. It will take you longer to process the task of reading it.[2] This phenomenon, captured in a famous experiment known as the Stroop Test, also arises in the Shout the Wrong Name game.

I swear I'm not mean in asking students—and you—to shout the wrong name. By trying to do something wrong, you've just practiced a skill that is vital for success with spontaneous communication: maximizing mediocrity.

Mediocrity usually gets a bad rap—and deservedly so. Nobody wants to maximize their mediocrity. But in spontaneous communication, that's exactly what you need to do. In a delightful paradox, the more mediocre you give yourself permission to be, the better, more compelling a speaker you become.

When handling tasks in daily life, we usually work hard to do them right. But with spontaneous communication, there is no "right," "correct," or "best" way. There are only better and worse ways. The very act of trying to "get it right" hampers us. It locks us in and overloads our minds, preventing us from responding to our listeners and projecting our personalities fully in the moment.

To do our best when put on the spot, we must stop aiming to deliver a perfect performance and instead become much more comfortable with getting things wrong. We must strive for mediocrity. In this chapter, I'll attempt to persuade you that embracing imperfect performance is the key to all successful spontaneous communication. Let's start by looking more closely at how our desire for excellence saps our communicative power.

The Shortcuts We Take on Our Way to Get It "Right"

Two distinct mental processes thwart us when we aim to "get it right" in spontaneous speaking. To understand the first of these, let's return to the Shout the Wrong Name game. I invite you to take another stab at it—again, fifteen or twenty seconds of pointing to objects and shouting out whatever word jumps to mind.

Are you finished? Good. This time, think about the words you shouted. Although the assignment was to shout out words at random, did you notice your brain consciously or unconsciously deploying a strategy to perform this task? Did the words you chose follow a pattern?

When my students play this game, they often report calling out words that belong to a common category. In quick succession, they'll point to objects and shout the names of fruits, animals, colors, and so on. Other students share that they borrow words used by others in the room, or that they use the real name of the previous object that they looked at. Some quickly think of several words with the idea that they'll use those for the next several objects to which they point.

As Adam Tobin highlights during his debriefs of this game, such strategies are perfectly normal, part of how our brains respond when we try to master challenging situations. Psychologists explain this via cognitive load theory, which holds that we often only have a finite amount of working memory to devote to the tasks before us.[3] When too much information barrages our brains all at once, as often occurs in our modern, tech-centered world, our working memory becomes overtaxed, and we struggle to learn. To avoid this outcome, our brains try to help us out. They quickly and effortlessly call up mental shortcuts, or *heuristics*, that allow us to solve problems and perform the tasks that confront us. Heuristics are a primary tool we deploy in our efforts to "get it right" and achieve perfection.[4]

We commonly rely on heuristics during spontaneous speaking. When an irate customer confronts us with a problem, our brains click in and we give a standard sort of reply, perhaps something like, "I'm sorry to hear that it's not working out for you. Did you set the product up properly?" When we learn of a friend's loss, we say, "My thoughts are with you." When a relative shares some bad news, we give a standard reply like, "I'm sure it will be okay." When a friend asks what we think of a difficult interaction they had with a coworker, we unthinkingly reply, "It is what it is."

Heuristics are essential in that they help us respond decisively and efficiently in complex situations, lightening the cognitive load we bear. Confronted with a task, we don't have to think about it—we just do it. If we lacked heuristics, we'd be stymied at every turn. Imagine how onerous we'd find it at the grocery store. We'd have to think through the pros and cons of every brand and variety of spaghetti sauce before choosing which one to buy. Instead, we apply a simple rule, something like, "I want a sauce that's organic and doesn't cost too much money."

The Surprising Power of "Because"

This efficiency, however, comes at a cost, in two key respects. First, heuristics limit our spontaneity, which interferes with our ability to be present. In a famous experiment, psychologist Ellen Langer had participants approach people waiting in line to use a photocopier and ask if they could cut in. The would-be line-cutter phrased their request in different ways, in some cases using the word "because" and offering a rationale. As she found, people waiting in line were far more likely to agree to let someone cut if they used the word "because" and offered a rationale. This held true regardless of whether the rationale was relatively strong ("I'm in a rush") or weak ("Excuse me, I have some copies to make. May I use the Xerox machine because I need to make copies?"). The word "because" apparently prompted people to go on autopilot, triggering a heuristic in their minds, perhaps something like, "I'll let someone cut in front of me if they have a reason." Rather than being present in the moment and listening carefully, one simple word justifying a small request triggered a tendency to behave mindlessly and distractedly.[5]

As a result, we don't take the time to slow down and observe nuances of our environment, and we miss subtle and perhaps not-so-subtle elements of it. If you're in the grocery store vetting spaghetti sauces on the basis of their price and whether they're organic, you might not notice whether some of them are a slightly different variety (say, chunky or vodka-infused) or if they have ingredients you don't want, such as added sugar. As a result, you might wind up making a decision you'll later find subpar.

When we deploy heuristics in interpersonal situations, we miss the nuances, including cues related to our audience members' needs. Let's say your colleague pops into your office and asks you unexpectedly for feedback on a meeting you were both just in. Your "give feedback on meeting" heuristic kicks in, and you immediately begin responding with an answer about next steps following the meeting, adjustments to plans, and other action items that were discussed. But your colleague might want something else—validation of their leadership ability, say, or maybe even just an expression of warmth or friendship on your part. You're so locked into the notion of "I must now say what I thought of that meeting" that you miss an opportunity to connect in a more meaningful way.

Effective spontaneous communication requires us to break out of our existing behavior patterns and ruts. Rather than hurry to respond to a situation, we must put a hold on heuristics, taking a moment to really assess the situation we're in and perhaps ask clarifying questions. In the above example, a nonheuristic induced response might lead us to ask something like, "Are you looking for feedback on the specifics of the meeting, or do you want me to tell you my general impressions?" Alternatively, we might ask our colleague what *they* thought about the meeting before sharing our opinion. Such questions might well yield information we can use to react more effectively.

Now, That's the Right Way to Eat Spaghetti!

Our use of heuristics poses a second problem: it limits our creativity. Because our brains are operating in rule-bound ways, we tend to arrive at answers that are expected, familiar, or logical. We are less likely to spontaneously generate reactions that are more creative, novel, or "out there." One of my favorite examples in this regard comes from a class my colleague Tina Seelig taught years ago to design students at Stanford.[6] Dividing her students into teams, she had them compete to arrive at the best, most innovative business idea. Each group had two hours and five dollars at their disposal. Using these resources, they had to earn as much money as possible (without breaking the law, of course). Afterward, each team would spend three minutes presenting their business idea in front of the class. The team that earned the most money would win the competition.

Most groups generated business ideas that were intriguing, but not especially mind-blowing. One group made quite a bit of money by making reservations in advance at popular restaurants and selling them to hungry diners (this is before the advent of online reservations services). Another group made a couple of hundred dollars by setting up a stand on the Stanford campus and offering to measure students' tire pressure and fill up their tires. At first, they charged for filling the tires, but they soon found that they earned more when they simply asked grateful students for a donation.

Another team took a whole different approach. These students reasoned that the most valuable resource they could sell wasn't their ability to perform a service for customers but rather to deliver a captive audience for companies wishing to recruit students for employment. To generate revenue, they sold their three minutes of presentation time to a design firm. They wound up earning $650, more money than any other team.

The other teams had followed a heuristic: "To make money, I've got to dream up some service customers would find attractive." But that heuristic locked them in, limiting the kinds of ideas they could generate. The winning team didn't follow that heuristic. As a result, they opened themselves up to ask a different set of questions: "What resource that I possess has the most value? And how can I best market *that*?"

Relying on heuristics might enable us to respond quickly when put on the spot, but we usually aren't opening ourselves up to many other, possible paths that might surprise or deeply engage our audiences. It is only when we manage to suspend and venture beyond our normal mental rules that magic can happen.

Some time ago, I had the privilege of teaching high school English for two years. If you want a setting where an ability to speak on the fly helps, this is it. Every day brought some new, unexpected communication challenge—I really had to stay on my toes.

In one of my classes, I had a supersmart kid who for some reason delighted in being disruptive in class. His tactic: he'd spontaneously and unpredictably blurt out random words and phrases during class discussions. I might be lecturing about *The Great Gatsby* when I'd hear a voice in the back of the room shouting something like, "My T-shirt is dirty" or "The pigeons scare me." The other kids found these bizarre interjections amusing. Me, not so much.

I knew this boy was trying to get attention, so I usually didn't respond to his outbursts. One day, I couldn't help myself. I had been eating lunch before class, and I happened to have a small packet of Parmesan cheese on my desk. Halfway through the class, the boy blurted out, "I love spaghetti." Everyone laughed. I desperately wanted this kid to keep quiet and behave. Spotting the cheese packet, I said, "Hey, catch," and tossed it to him. "Now, that's the right way to eat spaghetti!"

It was a spontaneous act of communication on my part, and it did the trick. Everyone laughed—they thought it was hilarious. We moved on with the lesson, and the boy kept quiet. Up until that point I had been following my standard teaching heuristic, such as "Ignore and move on," or "Stop the class, chastise the boy for being disruptive, and threaten him with a consequence if he doesn't comply." But in that moment, I thought of an entirely different and unexpected way of navigating the situation, one that expressed my own personality and sense of humor. My class loved it, and students came to see me in a different light—as a teacher with whom they could relate and engage with in a more authentic way.

Hack Your Heuristics

To up our communications game, we don't need to banish in full our every use of heuristics. Rather, we want to become more aware of the mental shortcuts we habitually take, learning to tune them out or turn them off at times so that we can become more agile and adaptive. We want to increase our ability to make conscious choices when we communicate rather than simply invoking a rote response.

One approach is to stay alert for situations in which we typically use heuristics. Usually, we resort to heuristics when we experience a stressor of some kind. We might face a decision and feel overwhelmed by the number of choices at our disposal. We might feel tired, hungry, or under a time crunch. We might find ourselves in an uncertain or ambiguous situation. To avoid using heuristics, we can prevent ourselves from becoming stressed in the first place. We can manage our stress once it does arise, taking care of ourselves in the moment, slowing down, or rationalizing (see chapter 1). Reducing the anxiety we feel can allow for more open and thoughtful engagement on our part.

We can also learn more about heuristics by observing others using them and trying to avoid those patterns. As parents, for instance, we might observe other parents always raising their voices when their children pummel them with requests. We can consciously focus on modifying our own behavior when our kids are nagging us—for instance, by slowing down, quieting our voices, and listening to our kids' requests.

We can also take time to reflect on our own actions. If we lead a team and are trying to communicate more productively when problems arise, we can make a habit each day of thinking back on how we handled these kinds of situations. Did we react reflexively in patterned ways? Did specific triggers spur these reactions? To what extent were these reactions helpful? What might we do in these situations to suspend our use of heuristics?

A final way to manage our mental shortcuts is to shake up how we think or act. Athletes who are right-handed often keep themselves on their toes by playing with their left hand or a ball that is heavier than normal. All of their ingrained habits go out the window, and they have to learn anew how to operate. I know a writer who purposely changes where he writes to free himself from ingrained thought patterns. While he usually works in his office, he has sometimes chosen to write in hospital waiting rooms, hotel lobbies, airports, funeral homes, empty movie theaters, and the spectator section of courtrooms. As he tells me, writing in new locations allows him to escape the same old patterns, unlocking a stream of new ideas.

Creativity experts likewise work proactively to short-circuit heuristic biases. When generating new ideas, design company IDEO deploys a technique of looking for inspiration in other, seemingly unrelated contexts where similar conditions or principles apply. In one instance, the company was hired to redesign a hospital emergency room so that it operates more efficiently. A standard approach would have been to research how great hospital emergency rooms were designed and to borrow ideas from them. Doing so, however, would have left IDEO's designers limited by whatever heuristic biases typically informed designers of emergency rooms.

Instead, IDEO considered other high-intensity environments to see how they functioned best.[7] One example they came upon was to investigate how Formula 1 race car pit crews performed. Pit crews were analogous to emergency room teams, IDEO proposed, in that both had to operate quickly and efficiently in high-pressure situations to diagnose and fix problems. Avoiding the usual hospital design heuristics and turning to pit crews for inspiration allowed IDEO to arrive at all kinds of new ideas it could translate into emergency rooms.

As an example, pit crews typically identify in advance the most common repair issues they'll have to deal with during a race. For each one, they assemble the needed parts and tools into a kit. That way, when a repair issue arises, they can fly into action without having to search around for parts and tools. IDEO introduced similar kits into emergency rooms to handle some of the most common scenarios that arise, such as drug overdoses or heart attacks. With this innovation, emergency rooms can operate more efficiently to treat patients. Breaking from the usual heuristics made all the difference.

We can all benefit from taking a break from our mental shortcuts. In doing so, we give ourselves space to be more responsive and potentially more creative in our communication.

● ● ● TRY IT ● ● ●

Take my seven-day "hack my heuristic" challenge. First, think of heuristics you often use when communicating. Maybe you start emails with "I hope you are well" or say "good question" when someone asks you something. For each day during the week, think of one action you will take to break with your heuristics. On a given day, you might identify a particular situation that you find stressful and take steps to manage your anxiety. You might build in a two-to-three-minute period to reflect on your behavior. Or you might think of a way to add an element of novelty that will allow you to break from your ingrained patterns.

The "Right" Wrong Name

Our use of heuristics isn't the only mental process that thwarts us when we aim to "get it right" in spontaneous speaking. To uncover a second one, let's once again return to Shout the Wrong Name. When I ask audience members about their experience playing this game, I often hear them beating up on themselves. They offer responses like "I failed," "I wasn't creative," "I did worse than so-and-so." Most strikingly, someone in the group will say, "I wasn't wrong enough." When I ask them to elaborate, they'll say something like, "Well, I was going to call this chair a cat, but both have four legs, and cats sit on chairs. I was not being wrong enough. I could have said, 'taco,' or 'Galápagos,' which are less similar to chairs."

Think about this response for a moment. The rules of this game are simply to shout the wrong name. I say nothing about how to define "wrong," nor do I impose criteria about which forms of being wrong are better or worse than others. The goal is not to compete or compare responses with others. Yet students try to play the game "right" by judging how well they are doing at being wrong.

Such self-evaluation serves us well in many situations—it's important in life to try to do our best. In fact, you'll get yourself fired at work or fail in your personal relationships if you don't judge and evaluate what you do or say. But in some circumstances—especially those that crop up spontaneously—fixating on monitoring and judging our performance *decreases* the likelihood that we'll do well. It taxes our cognitive capacities, preventing us from being as focused, creative, confident, and responsive as we'd like. It even can prevent us from taking action at all.

I once had a student who, while playing Shout the Wrong Name, just stood pointing at the same object repeatedly. He tried to utter a name, but nothing came out. When I asked what he was doing, he said he just couldn't come up with "the right wrong name." He was evaluating every potential name that popped into his brain, checking it against his own internal rulebook. None of them measured up to some standard he had established for himself.

It's not hard to understand why we judge ourselves so much, sometimes to the point of becoming perfectionistic. Many of us grow up saturated in a culture that emphasizes performance. Parents, teachers, mentors, bosses, coaches, and others pound in the message that there is a right way to do things, and doing it right is good. All our lives, we've received rewards for performing tasks correctly, winning praise, trophies, money, and fancy titles. We've received punishments for messing up, whether it's negative feedback, poor grades, or simply an awareness that others are looking down on us. Failing feels bad, while doing it right feels good. No surprise we're constantly monitoring and critiquing how we do, perhaps more than we should.

Another reason we're quick to judge our own performance is that doing so calms us and affords us a sense of control. Unpredictable and ambiguous situations in life can leave us feeling vulnerable and exposed. Focusing and sometimes obsessing over performing tasks perfectly can give us a sense of agency. Before major meetings, I often found myself fixating on exactly what I intended to say. I now realize this was an attempt to give myself a sense of control over my destiny when what was likely to unfold was out of my hands.

Of course, suspending perfectionism requires that we believe in our ability to accomplish our goals. It's precisely this faith that I'm asking you to muster. I assure you that it will be rewarded handsomely. After encouraging my students and other audience members to suspend self-judgment, I ask them to repeat the Shout the Wrong Name game. Most of them experience the game differently this time around. The smiles on their faces are bigger. They move more quickly around the room and point to objects more readily. They have less trouble coming up with names and enjoy themselves more.

We don't often allow ourselves to just *live* without worrying about how we're doing. But we should.

Dare to Be Dull

How do we stop from judging ourselves so much? One big technique that is surprising in its simplicity is that we can give ourselves permission to do what needs to be done. Nothing more, nothing less—rather than striving to do it right, we focus only on relaying the information we have to our audience.

This technique is actually a core tenet in the world of improvisation. Great improvisers get over the hump of their perfectionist tendencies by telling themselves that "good enough is great" and that they should "dare to be dull."[8] As they know, the more we can dare to be dull, the greater the chances we'll be anything *but* dull—because we will be communicating using our full cognitive resources. "'Be obvious' is the most powerful, creative mantra that there is," improvisation expert Dan Klein told me. "When you're trying to be original, you sound like everyone else trying to be original. But when you're obvious, you're yourself. And that's what's genuine."[9]

Entertainment executive Steve Johnston served as president and managing partner of comedy icon Second City for almost twenty years and now helps run Mindless Inc. an academy that uses applied and free-style improvisation methods to enhance mental fitness. He observes that we tend to think we must come up with the Big Idea when we speak, contributing something important, beautiful, or transcendent—what he likens to a cathedral. But providing the building block of a conversation—the brick—also matters. We serve as bricks by waiting, listening, and at times offering up logical connections between others' ideas. We don't have to say something original or pathbreaking every time. It's enough—and sometimes uniquely powerful—to help keep a conversation going and connect the pieces. Don't strive to be a cathedral. Focus on being as useful a brick as you can be.

Cultivating dullness can feel odd at first, even a little scary. When I invite Stanford students to dare to be dull, they look at me and gasp.

Nobody in their lives has ever told them to do this. But suspending judgment and ceding a bit of control is precisely what these students require to do better with spontaneous communication. They already have intelligence, motivation, and diligence. The next step for them to improve their communication is to take some of the precious cognitive resources they were spending in the dogged pursuit of perfection and redirect them to being present and engaged in the task at hand. This shift takes effort at first, which seemingly contradicts my point that this is about using less energy. But students find that their communication does become smoother and more authentic with practice.

Remember, there's no right or wrong way to communicate, only better and worse ways. Shifting from doing it right to just doing it reduces the pressure we feel. It allows us to focus less on the best possible way of communicating and simply allows us to put things in our own words and terms. Our communication becomes easier, less cognitively demanding, and more unique to us. We can focus on what needs to be done rather than diverting some of our bandwidth to judging what we're doing.

● ● ● TRY IT ● ● ●

Take a minute to think about a successful spontaneous communication or two you've had—a time when you simply did what was needed and didn't monitor and evaluate your performance unduly. What did this feel like afterward? Remind yourself that you *can* do this well and so should trust yourself to adopt a "dare to be dull" mindset.

Make Missed-Takes

Once we've granted ourselves permission to engage without obsessing over our performance, we can begin to free ourselves of the pressure to avoid making errors.

To embrace mistakes, we can learn to adjust how we think of them—not as the opposite of success, but as the means to it. When

Stanford marketing professor S. Christian Wheeler appeared on my podcast, he remarked that mistakes and failures are a natural and essential part of the learning process. As toddlers and small children, we think nothing of making mistakes. We're always messing up the simplest of tasks—walking, using a spoon, tying our shoes. As adults, we distance ourselves from failure, and in turn, prevent ourselves from learning and growing. "We need to recognize that failure is a great thing," Wheeler says, "because failure suggests that we are operating at the outside of our abilities and that we have some skills that we can acquire to better adapt to our circumstances."[10]

We can actively dial down our reflexive judging and evaluation by making a choice to practice accepting and even embracing mistakes when they happen. Stressing over every little mistake we make—or might make—is mentally taxing. I find it helpful to envision mistakes as "missed takes" in the making of a film. When a crew films a scene, they will often do several versions or "takes." They might do a close-up instead of a distant shot, have the actors stand instead of sit, have them modulate their tone, and so on. They do this not because any one take is right or wrong, but because the director and crew want to broaden their options and make sure they didn't miss any potentially great but unforeseen ways of rendering the scene. They seek out variety—takes that might be more creative, unique, or imaginative.

We can think of our communication situations as opportunities to try out possible approaches (more on this in the next chapter). When we take the pressure off each interaction, each encounter becomes just another "take" among many, one that helps illuminate what better communication might look like. Mistakes in this vein can focus our efforts. Rather than diminishing us, they can empower us and put us on a path to become better communicators.

Reframing errors as "missed-takes" can be incredibly powerful, and not just in communication. As an avid practitioner of martial arts, I once went through a period when I hit a wall—metaphorically, not physically—and didn't know what to do. I had reached a certain level of proficiency, but I wasn't improving further. A big problem, it turned out, was the way I was punching. In my drive to deliver the ideal punch,

I was moving my body in a way that limited the power of my punches. My punches might have looked good, but they lacked enough oomph.

To solve this problem, I allowed myself to focus on missed-takes. Deviating from what I thought was the perfect form, I experimented with different ways of moving my body while punching. With each shot, I noted how I felt and the results I obtained. Some of my adjustments didn't help—I would feel pain in places where I wasn't supposed to, or the force of my punch would remain the same or even decline. I set aside each missed-take and experimented with other adjustments. Over time, as these experiments continued, I discovered a way of aligning my body while punching that allowed for much more force. My form wasn't perfect in conventional terms, but it worked for me. Only when I began to view mistakes as invaluable parts of a larger learning process did I improve.

In professional contexts, we can accept or welcome in mistakes by publicly celebrating failures and working systematically to learn from them. A software company where I worked held what they called "Failure Fridays." Each Friday, the whole company would enjoy a free lunch together. Individuals would take a few minutes to share a failure they had experienced, and leaders would bestow an award for the "best" failure. The point was to normalize failures so as to encourage risk-taking and also to encourage teams to learn from mistakes. Critically, the winning failure couldn't be one that others had already made. Failures were valuable, but only if we took the time to learn from them.

● ● ● TRY IT ● ● ●

Think of a common communication you regularly deliver, such as a weekly status update or a virtual check-in. Challenge yourself to try different takes. You might vary your emotion, changing your vocal intensity, reframing a statement as a question, inviting others to speak first, injecting humor, adjusting your body posture, and so on.

Conversations, Not Performances

Whether we realize it or not, many of us approach certain spontaneous interactions as we do formal speaking situations—as performances. When meeting people for the first time, making small talk, or speaking in front of a larger group than you normally would be comfortable with, we can feel as if we're onstage before an audience. This can happen even if that audience is only one or two people whose presence adds pressure to a situation. We presume that this audience is critically assessing our every move, judging it according to some set of rules and expectations. This perception on our part ratchets up the pressure, leading us to monitor and assess ourselves in an attempt to please our audience.

Think about areas in our lives in which we typically perform: perhaps we play a musical instrument, or play on a softball team, or act onstage. In these settings, everyone's eyes are on us. There's a right way and a wrong way to behave. If we hit a wrong note, drop a ball in the infield, or forget our lines, the error is clear to all. Some sports actually keep track of how many flubs players have made.

We can also relax more by reframing spontaneous interaction as *conversations* rather than performances. Conversations are more casual and familiar than performances. We usually don't rehearse for conversations—we just have them. We usually don't think in terms of mistakes—we just try to sustain a flow and connection. Although conversations can be uncomfortable at times and we might still feel judged, these feelings are much less pronounced than in performance situations. We can relax and just be ourselves.

To help us reframe communications as conversations, we can take three steps. First, we can *adjust our use of language.* When we feel ourselves to be on a stage, or at least in the spotlight, we sometimes use words that are cold, formal, and passive. We do this because we're anxious and seek to establish authority. Otherwise, we might get physical distance by stepping back and folding our hands in front of us.

Let's say you're a doctor, and you're standing in front of a group of your peers. You might find yourself making statements like, "It is imperative that doctors help solve this problem." Language like this creates distance between yourself and others. When you say, "*We* must solve this problem," you are not only speaking more simply and economically, but more persuasively. The word "we" is more inclusive. The communication feels more direct—more like an informal conversation. When you use language like this, your audience members might begin to do so as well. Your joint sense of the interaction as a performance dissipates, and you become more connected with one another. You get closer to actually solving the problem simply by directly pointing out that it is all of yours to solve.

Another way of reframe communication as conversation is by *posing more questions.* Questions, even rhetorical ones, are two-way interactions. You and others around you enter into a back-and-forth. No longer are you alone "onstage" in front of your audience—you're engaging in a dialogue. Even when you're making a statement, you can think of it as an answer to an unasked question. That in itself can give the encounter a conversational feel and lower the pressure you might experience.

Answering your own unasked questions can help ease pressure in formal speaking situations as well. One distinguished academic I know, a Nobel laureate, wanted to improve his public speaking, which he regarded as good but a bit stiff. He began structuring them around important research questions, using these questions as the titles of his slides. These in turn served as cues to relay his intended content; he simply provided the answers to his questions for his audience. The technique makes his presentations more connected and conversational, allowing him to feel more relaxed. He doesn't worry about presenting his every idea in a pre-planned way that his audience will perceive as elegant or perfect. He's just speaking casually with his audience members, asking questions they might have and answering them.

Finally, we must *beware of the memorization trap* into which so many of us fall. In advance of job interviews or other situations where we'll likely have to speak spontaneously, it is tempting to have some key lines or talking points nailed down in advance. That way, we'll know just what to say when the time comes.

Writing down what we might want to say can help, but memorization also can come back to haunt us. Giving our communication the feel of a formal, over-rehearsed presentation, it can ratchet up our nerves as we struggle to remember a great zinger that we'd thought of in advance of the actual conversation. We wind up scrutinizing what we're saying, paying attention to every little deviation from our script and framing it as a mistake. Also, by taking valuable mental energy to remember our lines, we inhibit our ability to react naturally to others around us. We have less cognitive capacity at our disposal to listen to others and react in kind.[11] We're in our heads, not where we should be—immersed in the social world.

Instead of rushing to memorize, try writing out what you'd like to say and then turning that into a short, bullet-pointed outline. Doing so allows you to think through the material in detail while giving you a brief structure that's easier to keep in mind. Using that structure, you can more confidently fill in the gaps as you go (more on structure in chapter 5).

Getting Out of Your Own Way

Advice	Explanation	Payoff
Be Alert to Heuristics	We usually deploy them in response to a stressor. Start noticing when you are hangry, tired, or annoyed.	When you reflect and slow down, you'll be more original and connected.
Dare to Be Dull	Don't focus on "doing it right"—take a hint from Nike and "Just Do It."	When you stop monitoring or prejudging your performance, attempting a perfect execution, you'll be more creative and freer.

Advice	Explanation	Payoff
Embrace Mistakes	Reframe failure as part of your journey to success.	Instead of thinking of your interaction as a failure, you'll be a movie star who just experienced a "missed take" while filming.
Converse	Remember that people aren't scrutinizing you as closely as you think (or really at all).	When we think of interactions as conversations instead of performances before a critical public, they'll flow more easily.
Choose Informality	To accomplish the "performances-to-conversations" reframe, adjust your use of language and make it more casual.	It's more intimate and endearing when you aren't so stiff.
Dialogue, Not Monologue	You aren't a "sage on a stage," so interact and ask some questions.	Life and communication are more fun, and successful, when it's a two-way street.
Extemporaneous Is Best	Resist the temptation to memorize and give yourself some cues or talking points instead.	You'll mentally tax yourself less and won't come across as so formal.

Reconnect with Your Spontaneous Self

Anthony Veneziale is a master of spontaneous communication. Since the early 2000s, he has been a member of Freestyle Love Supreme, the Tony Award–winning improvisational comedy troupe he cofounded with actor Lin-Manuel Miranda. He also cofounded the communication training firm Mindless Inc. and FLS Academy, an organization dedicated to "fostering diverse creative voices using improvisation and freestyle rap."[12] If there's anyone who knows how to communicate well when put on the spot, it's Veneziale (and if you doubt me, just check out his 2019 improvised TED Talk, created on the spot using PowerPoint slides he hadn't seen before).[13] For him, impromptu speaking isn't merely an interesting pastime or even a career. It's a way of life.

Veneziale is the last person you'd think would have ever been nervous when put on the spot. But there was a time in his life when speaking spontaneously was incredibly difficult and anxiety-producing for him. As a child, Veneziale had a severe speech impediment that prevented him from pronouncing the letters *r* and *w*. His four older brothers teased him mercilessly about it, leaving him shy and afraid to express himself. He stayed quiet, fearing the failure and social ostracism he might experience each time he opened his mouth.

Veneziale overcame his speech impediment by working with a speech therapist who would challenge him to take risks with his speaking—such as speaking up in class, volunteering to go first, or asking a clerk for assistance—and then reward him with small treats or action figures. By middle school, as a result of this "low-risk exposure therapy," he felt more confident as a speaker, so much so that he auditioned for the school play. "I was like, 'I can do this now. I can say 'root beer.' It's not 'woot beer' anymore. My mouth isn't sort of filled with marbles, which is how it used to feel as a kid." He became even more comfortable and playful as a speaker, eventually joining an improvisational comedy troupe in college. Small, gradually increasing exposures to spontaneous speaking made a profound difference.

We should acknowledge that the fear of failure likely looms larger for some of us than for others. If we belong to a traditionally underrepresented group, we might feel marginalized or shoulder the extra pressure of representing our group to the outside world. With the stakes that much higher, failure seems even scarier. Depending on our personal histories and past experiences, we might experience imposter syndrome, a fear that we don't belong and can't perform as expected.

Let me be clear: you *do* belong and your contributions *are* valuable.

Vivek Venugopal, vice president of sales at Mindless Inc., advises that we reflect on the unique perspective we bring to any communications challenge, whether formal or spontaneous. He urges us to be ourselves and to remember, "The reason that you have been asked to travel around the world and speak. The reason that you've been asked to speak at this wedding. The reason that you are in this one-on-one conversation. It's not because of your title. It's because of the sum total of all the experiences in your life that have brought you here. Embrace them and bring them in."[14]

I firmly believe that all of us have greatness inside of us as spontaneous speakers. We just have to stop getting in our own way. Instead of constricting our personalities, masking our individual thoughts and ideas with formalities, we have to set ideas free and reconnect with our spontaneous selves. As my experienced improvisor friends remind us, our daily lives are spontaneous. None of us go about our days rigidly following a prearranged script or plan (okay, maybe a few highly programmed politicians do, but not the rest of us ordinary folks). We *know* how to be spontaneous.[15] Our task is simply to manage our fears and practice spontaneity in our social interactions.

● ● ● DRILL IT ● ● ●

1. The next time you're in a meeting, observe how you tend to respond. What mental shortcuts do you use? For instance, do you tend to say "good idea" to ingratiate yourself with your colleagues when they make suggestions? When you present ideas and field audience questions, do you say "good question" after each query to buy yourself time in

order to think? Identify three mental shortcuts you take. For each one, reflect on other ways you might respond that are more spontaneous. Experiment with these alternatives in upcoming meetings.

2. After your next spontaneous exchange with someone, spend a few minutes reflecting. Consider all of the self-judgments you rendered in the course of the encounter. Are you harsher on yourself than you realized? Do your judgments and evaluations reveal a pattern? Did your judgments enhance your communication in the moment or make it more difficult?

3. Think about communication failures you've experienced as well as how these failures have affected you. As painful as those failures might have been, did they also confer important benefits? What vital lessons did you learn?

Chapter 3: Redefine

MIND YOUR MINDSET

You can take back control when put on the spot.
It's all about how you see it.

Most people dislike the experience of getting lost in an unfamiliar place. They see it as an inconvenience, a waste of time, perhaps even a threat to their personal safety. And so they switch on their GPS, allowing it to guide them. With a computer telling them where to go, they need never fear that they'll lose their bearing and veer off into the unknown. They pay less attention to the surroundings they pass along the way because they are only concerned with their destination, and not their journey.

My friend Dan Klein, improvisation expert and lecturer at Stanford, takes a different approach. He goes out for a walk or a jog and *tries* to get lost. As he recounted on my podcast, he doesn't try "to get so lost that it's actually physically dangerous and I might be in trouble."[1] Just a little lost, for the sake of discovering something new and potentially wonderful.

Once Klein was out jogging in his Bay Area neighborhood and decided to go on a small adventure. Having recently moved to the area, he had become accustomed to running along a nearby bike path. On a whim, he turned right at an intersection just to see what he would find. Scarcely had he gone half a block when he discovered a trailhead, smack dab in the middle of the city. He'd passed the spot before but never noticed it.

Entering the trail, he found himself in a small urban park, a hidden oasis of native plants. "I found myself instantly transported," he says, "not just from the visuals of the native flora, but from the smell. It was this incredible native Californian olfactory explosion."[2]

He lingered for a few moments to take in his surroundings and appreciate nature's beauty. It was a memorable and enriching experience, one he never would have enjoyed had he not taken a small risk and deviated from his routine. From then on, he made this small park a regular part of his pre-workout warm-up. He takes a deep breath, drinking in the scents from the plants, "and then I'm ready to go."

When we suspend our usual expectations and goals and greet the world with a spirit of openness, curiosity, and adventure, we can benefit in unforeseen ways. It's true with getting lost, and it's true with spontaneous speaking. By shifting our mindset, we can train ourselves to greet impromptu interactions not as threats but as opportunities for learning, collaboration, and growth. With this shift, we can see better results as communicators and learn to actually enjoy the journey.

The stress of spontaneous communication often leads us to see it as inherently threatening—a crucible in which we must defend and protect ourselves. We expend so much energy preparing to defend our ideas that we have less to expend on communicating creatively and passionately. We also begin to send a number of emotional or physical signals that all is not well. Our thinking becomes defensive rather than inclusive. Physically, we retreat to a defensive posture, sometimes literally stepping back or hiding behind a chair, turning our camera off, folding our arms in front of us, or slouching. Our breath might quicken, our vocal cords tighten, and our voice become shriller. Our tone might come across as defensive—rushed, curt, bothered, harsh—and the messages we convey can become clipped, noninclusive, distancing, and closed.

By reframing spontaneous communication as an opportunity rather than a threat, we can relax, let our personalities shine, and even have fun. Our focus expands as we entertain new and varied possibilities. We make our bodies physically bigger and more open, drawing closer to others and projecting a more intimate and engaging presence. Our tone sounds more confident, competent, and measured, and our messages become more empathetic, detailed, inclusive, and engaging. All of these changes can in turn trigger a virtuous cycle. As we relax more, engage, and enjoy ourselves, we invite others around us to do the same. Their positivity, openness, and curiosity nudge ours along even further.

Now, it's only fair to acknowledge that the stakes of different conversations can vary. In job interviews, competitive sales pitches, academic debates, and many other contexts, we might well encounter people who are gunning for us—I know I have. In our fractious times, it can seem like skeptical and even hostile audiences are the norm, especially in online venues. Yet those are exactly the situations where your communication skills become all the more useful. Not only that: we can reframe our perception of these "threats" to actually help us in surprising ways.

Many of us live in fear of encountering detractors or hecklers. We worry that they will distract us, throw us off course, make us look silly, or point out a flaw in our logic. Trevor Wallace, a comedian and social media sensation, embraces disruptive moments in which audience members challenge him. As he explains, these moments are unique—they have a magic to them that will never be replicated. Rather than attempting to quickly move on, he sometimes stays with these moments, asking questions of the heckler to see where they lead. Often, Wallace winds up with wildly entertaining stories that he never would have uncovered otherwise. Many of these extended moments have been so good that Wallace has posted them on social media to further expand his audience.[3]

We, too, can reap unforeseen benefits by greeting disruptive, spontaneous moments in our lives rather than rushing past them. In the vast majority of occasions, all of us have at least some ability to open ourselves up to possibility and opportunity. Even if people interrupt us maliciously, we would do well to engage these folks as fully and authentically as possible. It all comes down to our mindset.

During an appearance on my podcast, Stanford psychologist and director of the Stanford Mind and Body Lab Alia Crum defined mindsets as "ways of viewing reality that shape what we expect, what we understand, and what we want to do."[4] With this definition in mind, I encourage students and clients to cultivate *four key mindset shifts*—changes in thinking and approach—that support and enhance an openness to the many opportunities spontaneous speaking often afford. Some of these shifts might be more familiar, others less so. Let's explore each in turn, as well as some techniques for making some helpful mindsets a more prominent fixture of our lives.

Mindset Shift #1:
From Fixed to Growth

The psychologist Carol Dweck has famously distinguished between two ways of understanding our own personalities and potential, what she terms *fixed* and *growth* mindsets. A fixed mindset regards our knowledge and ability as fundamentally unchangeable. Either we have them, or we don't. A growth mindset sees our intelligence and capabilities as more fluid—skills can be learned, performance can be improved, minds can be changed.

If we embrace a fixed mindset, we spend time trying to prove our intellectual capacity to ourselves. We often try to avoid challenging situations, we don't feel motivated to better ourselves, we don't welcome critical feedback to help us change, and we treat others' success as a threat to our own. Adopting a growth mindset, by contrast, sparks a desire to learn and grow. We welcome challenges, alert to what they might teach us. We welcome critical feedback, and we try hard, believing that with diligence and persistence we can make progress. Instead of fearing others' success as a threat, we feel inspired by their examples and try to learn from them.

Dweck's work spotlights the tremendous benefits that come with thinking about ourselves as dynamic, changeable beings. People who do so tend to succeed more than those who are more fixed in their self-concept. This seems true for communication in particular. One study found that people who thought about themselves as capable of growth and positive change were less anxious about public speaking, perceived themselves to be better at it, and thought more deeply about public speaking and its impact.[5]

A growth mindset affirms the idea that impromptu communication is one of many opportunities for learning. If you bring to social interactions the notion that you are still incomplete as a human being and can improve, you'll probably feel more curious, engaged, and open-minded as you communicate. You won't feel as stressed if your communication doesn't go as planned; you'll regard any failures as a chance to practice your skills and learn valuable lessons. Without the need to prove or validate your abilities, you'll feel less pressured or besieged.

You can take a number of steps to help a growth mindset figure more prominently in your life (beyond reading Dweck's book and watching her TED Talk, which I highly recommend).[6] Adopting and honing a growth mindset involves focusing on the effort you put in rather than the results you obtain. If you've invested time and energy in working with your AMP (Anxiety Management Plan, discussed in chapter 1), give yourself credit for that! In social situations, remind yourself you have value to contribute and new insights to glean from your efforts. Try repeating a mantra to this effect—something like "I have something important to say and to learn."

In instances when you've struggled to communicate well, adopt what Dweck calls a "not yet" attitude. You can potentially master various aspects of spontaneous communication; you just haven't done it *yet*. Set realistic goals and delineate steps to achieve them. Take stock of your current proficiency and consider what kind of growth might be possible in the short and long term. Remind yourself that you might well achieve the improvement you seek if you keep trying, and that even if your progress is slow, trying your best has value in and of itself.

A "not yet" attitude also might lead you to pose helpful questions of yourself that could spur improvement. If you felt flustered during a question and answer session, you might ask yourself: How might I remind myself to breathe deeply and slowly in Q&A situations? What heuristics might be getting in my way during Q&A? What mantra might I use to remind myself that Q&A is an opportunity for missed takes?

As you achieve specific communication goals, focus on the journey you've been on rather than the destination you're attempting to reach. Visualize your goals as a path or a mountain to climb, using language like "process" or "adventure" to evoke an open-ended journey. Take notes along the way, reviewing your insights and observations period-ically to remind yourself of the process, including the highs and lows you experienced.[7] As research by Szu-chi Huang and Jennifer Aaker suggests, adopting a journey metaphor inclines us to continue the work we've done so far in support of a goal.[8]

● ● ● **TRY IT** ● ● ●

Consider a spontaneous speaking skill you would like to hone or improve, such as answering questions, giving a toast, or recovering from a mistake. What reasonable steps might you take to work on these skills? How might you focus your efforts in small increments to develop the skills you want? What steps have you already taken? What went well and what could be improved? Whom can you turn to for assistance?

Mindset Shift #2:
From Thinking about You to Thinking about Your Audience

When we perceive spontaneous communication situations as threatening, we're directing our attention onto ourselves. *We're* the ones under siege. *We're* the ones who seemingly have to prove ourselves—or else. As we go about addressing this threat, we continue to focus our attention squarely and narrowly on us—how we're behaving, what we're saying. To the extent we focus on others, we obsess over how they're reacting to us.

We can break this dynamic and embrace an opportunity mindset by shifting our focus away from ourselves and toward the audience. Who are they, really? What do they care about? How are they feeling right now? What do they want and need from us? Posing such questions, we can become aware of our situation as an opportunity to enhance the lives or experience of others. Depending on our content and the context at hand, we can empower, equip, educate, entertain, or inspire audience members with our remarks.

Patricia Ryan Madson, an improvisation expert who serves as professor emerita at Stanford, notes that when she teaches improvisation, the first thing she tells students is that improvisation is "not about you. It's about the rest of the people here and how you can work with them and how we're going to make something together here."[9] She's not alone in conveying this wisdom. Across all of the podcast interviews I've done, one of the ideas my guests return to most often is the importance of focusing on the audience. We do better if we regard spontaneous communication as an opportunity to render service to others and to learn and grow ourselves in the process. Making this mental shift allows us to take the pressure off ourselves and focus, in effect, on a higher pursuit.

To help us become more audience-centric, Madson suggests that we begin scrutinizing audience members and the physical environment the minute we walk into a room. "Really become the expert," she says, "not on your subject, but on this particular gathering and what's going on here." She notes that in formal speaking situations the information she gleans from studying her audiences has led her to alter her planned remarks. Perhaps the setting was surprisingly beautiful or she noticed some other feature relating to her audience on which she simply had to comment. In spontaneous situations, surveying the room can likewise yield a wealth of information, including the mood of audience members, their energy levels, their likes and dislikes, and so on. These insights can clue us in to what audience members expect of us and how we might best help them.

● ● ● TRY IT ● ● ●

The next time you attend a meeting, cocktail party, or some other situation where you might have to speak impromptu, take a moment at the outset to observe the social context. Pay attention to who is interacting with whom, where in the room people are located, who is most or least distracted or animated, and the general vibe. Notice environmental details such as the lighting, the furniture, the temperature, and so on. You'll be surprised when you realize how much information you can gather that will help you feel more at home.

In thinking about our audiences, we can remind ourselves that in most cases those communicating with us *want* us to succeed. Despite what it might seem, few people like to witness social awkwardness in others. Our audiences would like nothing better than to have a smooth, successful, and enjoyable interaction with us. As Madson puts it, "Unlike an Olympic judge who may be scanning the performance for the tiniest error, an audience (be it at a presentation, a meeting, or a performance) is a gaggle of humans, just like you; they are there to cheer you on and learn from you. We forget this when our mind creates disaster scenarios of our upcoming presentations."[10]

Imagine that the scenario is flipped and you are in the audience's shoes while someone else is in yours: Would *you* want to see a person flounder? If you had invited someone to an event, scheduled a meeting, or started a conversation, would you want the other person to feel uncomfortable or unable to express themselves? Of course not. What *would* you want to know if you were listening to yourself? What kind of experience would you want to have? What kind of information or message would you find relevant to our lives?

Google executive Kathy Bonanno believes that most audience members harbor a simple desire in posing questions of speakers: to "have a good moment" with the speaker, a heightened sense of connection and immediacy. When she handles audience questions, she focuses simply on trying to have such moments. This mental technique, she says, "has really relaxed me quite a bit. I'm just really trying to engage with them and connect with them."[11] Judging from the positive feedback she has received, the tactic works.

Focusing on the audience experience doesn't mean we should neglect ourselves; it simply means that we will feel more at ease in front of our audiences if we have a clear expectation of what will create a good moment. For instance, if a friend requests advice or feedback, ask for some relevant context about what type of response they are hoping to get and what specific concerns they want your thoughts on. By understanding our audiences, we can behave more authentically with them and ultimately serve them better. The effort on our part to do so will orient us away from a defensive posture and toward an openness to what we and our audiences might experience and accomplish together.

Last, when thinking about what you need to succeed, consider what your optimal circumstances might look like. Just as caregivers of any kind must take care of themselves first before they can care for others, so we must make sure we have what we need in any given moment to communicate at our best. Vivek Venugopal of the communications training firm Mindless Inc. advises people to "embrace their inner diva." As he notes, divas "know what they need to perform at their best, and they have the confidence to ask for it." If you're asked to give an impromptu toast or tribute and you need to feel as if your audience is paying attention, ask them kindly if they might put away their devices. If you want your audience to be involved and engaged, let them know that this interaction isn't going to be one-way, with you talking and them listening. Be honest and direct with your audience, and you'll be better off and so will they.

● ● ● TRY IT ● ● ●

Think about the speakers in different contexts whom you most admire. Who is the best presenter you've ever heard and what was so good about them? Who are your favorite conversation-alists and meeting leaders, and which of their behaviors appeal to you the most? Make a list of tactics and actions and consider how you might incorporate some of them into your own sponta-neous communication.

Mindset Shift #3:
From "Yes, But . . ." or "No!" to "Yes, And . . ."

Surprise—I have a gift for you! It's another game to play. For this one, you need a partner. If you're sitting at home, ask your spouse, child, or roommate to play it with you. If you're at work reading during your lunch break, ask a colleague to serve as your partner. If you're alone, jump on a virtual call. What I'd like you and your partner to do is to practice giving an imaginary gift to one another.

Your partner will give you a gift first. Ask them to hold out their hands in front of them as if they were giving you a big box wrapped up nice and tied with a bow. Your job is to pretend to receive the gift. You take the box, open it, look inside, and say, "Oh, this is wonderful. Thank you for the [fill in what the gift is]." Just utter the first thing that comes to your mind as the imaginary gift. It could be a baby rhinoceros. A lightbulb. A bar of bath soap. A stinky running shoe. Whatever it is, thank your partner for giving it. Your partner in turn will then explain on the spot why they got you the gift, saying whatever comes to their mind.

You might open the box and exclaim, "Oh, thank you so much for the turtle!" Your partner might in turn say, "Oh, yes, I knew you would like it because you were such a big fan growing up of Teenage Mutant Ninja Turtles. And what's better than having your very own live turtle?" This game thus has two bits of spontaneity built into it: first, in defining the gift; second, in justifying the giving of it.

Try giving the gift, and play this game again, with you serving as the giver. Isn't it fun to receive gifts, even if they're made up? When audience members at my presentations and workshops play this game with one another, they're usually quite joyful—they're laughing, smiling, nodding at one another, having fun. They're really *connecting* with one another.

This improv game was one of the first I ever played, and it remains one of my favorites. In the hands of master improvisers like Adam Tobin and Dan Klein, it can lead to all kinds of remarkable moments. I expose you to it for two reasons. First, it evokes this chapter's basic theme. What would it be like if we viewed our faux pas or questions others lobbed at us in the moment as opportunities and gifts rather than challenges and threats? Wouldn't that be amazing? Wouldn't the experience become a lot more fun and engaging? And wouldn't we connect much more profoundly with others around us?

The game also dramatizes a more specific mindset shift that helps support the notion of spontaneous speaking as an opportunity. So often in life, we resist ideas others put to us. If we don't say "no" outright, we might find ourselves saying some version of, "Yes, but . . ." As in, "Yes, that seems like a good idea, but you might want to think about this." Or, "Yes, I hear you, but I just don't think you're right." We object, critique, offer caveats.

In this game, we're doing none of that. Rather, we're validating what our partners say, and they in turn are validating our spontaneous responses. Each of the gift receivers says something silly when naming the gift. By going with it, their partner accepts exuberantly their contribution. They don't respond critically, saying something like "I didn't get you that." Instead of "Yes, but . . ." they respond with, "Yes, and . . ."

The concept of "Yes, and . . ." is a central tenet of improvisation.[12] Minute to minute, we wrench ourselves away from a critical sensibility and instead focus on affirming what our partner has said and building upon it. Under this approach, there are no right or wrong answers. There are only new and next answers. For each one, we can say "yes" and then tack on our own, unique contribution.

"Yes, and . . ." is both breathtakingly simple and extraordinarily powerful. Focus on "Yes, and . . ." in your daily encounters with others and you'll start to see each moment as an opportunity for something wonderful and unexpected. By adopting a posture of "Yes, and . . ." you nudge yourself to listen to what others are saying so that you can respond (I'll have more to say about listening in chapter 4). You also relinquish a measure of control over how a social interaction progresses. You can't plot out each step in advance. All you can do is listen and respond and then continue to add to subsequent contributions others make. Each contribution you make becomes an opportunity to take the conversation in a new and interesting direction.

You can take a number of steps to embrace a posture of "Yes, and . . ." in impromptu speaking situations. First, seek out areas of alignment with others, even if you are in conflict or are negotiating. Try to take areas of agreement as your starting point and return to these areas periodically as your conversation develops. You might find that efforts to find common ground—to say "yes"—open up space for others around you to do the same, enabling a positive dynamic to take root.

I have benefited from using "Yes, . . . and," to help me in a number of challenging conversations. By noting areas of agreement, I have found that I can reframe my discussions in a new, open way that leads to more creative resolutions. Once, I helped two of my regional managers deal with a conflict over hiring a trainer or a customer support person. After hearing arguments for why they each should get the new hire for their team, I highlighted that we all agreed on our most pressing needs, and that we had an opportunity to reenvision training as pro-active customer support allowing us to leverage the headcount for a new, hybrid role.

● ● ● **TRY IT** ● ● ●

The next time you experience tension or conflict in a conversation with someone, pause for a few seconds to make a quick mental list of your points of agreement. Once you've thought of a few items, guide the conversation toward one of these areas of agreement to help kick off a "Yes, and . . ." dynamic.

"Yes, and . . ." is an incredibly helpful way of slowing down your judgment of an idea. Instead of allowing your first response to dictate your reaction, use "Yes, and . . ." to tease out the underlying logic. Although it might seem difficult at first to say "Yes, and . . . ," such a response might seem more plausible and natural as you understand the nuance of the other person's message and the context in which they formed their thoughts. Pay special attention to your own biases. It's easy to unintentionally squelch others' willingness to contribute by judging them too hastily. Likewise, when you interrupt someone or respond too quickly to a suggestion of theirs, they can feel ignored or undervalued. Adam Tobin in our Improvisationally Speaking class often reminds students that by purposely resisting the impulse to judge, you can not only open yourself up to new ideas but also ensure that you remain receptive to a variety of diverse ideas and inputs.

Mindset Shift #4:
From Dwelling on What Happened to "Next Play"

In her powerful book *Improv Wisdom*, Patricia Ryan Madson recounts how Stanford University once asked her to perform a reading at a commencement ceremony in front of one thousand people, including several dignitaries. Ahead of her in the program was a musical performance by the university's symphony orchestra. When the piece concluded, she was supposed to step up on the dais in her cap and gown and read a passage from Jane Stanford, the university's founder.

On the day of the event, Madson waited for the orchestra to finish. When it seemed like it had, she stood up, went to the podium, and said, "And now, the words of Jane Stanford." But to her great mortification, the orchestra began playing again. Madson had blown her cue: the orchestra was supposed to play two movements, not one. Laughter rippled through the audience. They could tell that she'd messed up.

Many of us might have panicked or froze in this situation. Not Madson. She went back to her seat and waited patiently. When the orchestra had completed the second movement, she went back up and repeated her opening line, "And *now*, the words of Jane Stanford."

Madson learned an important lesson about how to handle mistakes: Don't ruminate on them. Just keep going. "When you have a gaffe," she says, "your attention should be on what comes next, rather than on, how did I do that?" If you do, you might find that your audience appreciates your fortitude. "I think some of our heroes are those people who are not cowed by something. The advice I'd give to students is it's not the mistake that matters. It's your recovery that you've got control over."[13]

Duke University's legendary basketball coach Mike Krzyzewski, or Coach K as he's often called, famously came up with the dictum, widely practiced in sports, of "next play." If you miss a shot in basketball, swing and miss in baseball, or throw an interception in football, you should quickly reset your mind and keep going. Focus on the task at hand rather than on what just happened. By the same token, if you sink a three-pointer, hit a grand slam, or throw a touchdown pass, you also should keep going. Performance is fluid. To do your best, you should try to stay focused on what's happening now and not allow what just happened to distract you, regardless of how devastating or wonderful it might be. As Krzyzewski once put it, "Whatever you have just done is not nearly as important as what you are doing right now."[14] Former Duke star and NBA professional Shane Battier reckoned that next play was "the most simple but eloquent lesson" that Krzyzewski taught his players.

For our purposes, next play is essentially about preparing ourselves to seize opportunity as it arises. When we're dwelling on the past, we aren't alert to the possibilities latent in the present moment. But if we can discipline ourselves to move quickly to the next play regardless of what just happened, then, we're "starting fresh, and it's time for the next opportunity, with energy, preparation, positivity, again and again and again and again and again."[15]

For many of us, shifting to a "next play" mindset might seem daunting—we're used to attaching emotionally to past outcomes, and we struggle to break that pattern. If that's the case, we can practice staying in the moment and moving on to the next play with a game that budding improvisers often learn called New Choice. They start performing a scene, and at various points in the scene, the organizer of the game shouts, "New choice!" The performers drop the current scene or choice they just made and begin a new one, uttering whatever snippets of dialogue come to them. You can play this game yourself, using a timer to ring at a given interval or by enlisting a friend to shout "new choice" repetitively at odd intervals. Doing this for even just a few minutes can help you become comfortable simply leaving what you're doing and moving on.[16]

The next time you find yourself in a spontaneous speaking situation where things aren't going as planned, don't dwell on it. Allow yourself a brief moment to feel emotion—then refocus and move on. Tie Kim, a volunteer youth coach who is one of the best at his craft, relates that he uses next play all the time in his professional life. Serving as a CFO at a nonprofit, he has presented in formal meetings and occasionally fumbled answers to impromptu questions lobbed his way. Although he feels an impulse to go back and somehow correct what he had said, his habitual adoption of next play leads him to let go of what had just happened and continue with the presentation.[17] As a result, his presentations tend to go better overall.

On one occasion shortly after the 2018 mass shooting at the Marjory Stoneman Douglas High School in Parkland, Florida, I was delivering a talk on the importance of hearing diverse viewpoints and perspectives. I felt passionate about my topic but became distracted thinking about the stories I'd heard about the young victims. Although I had sketched out my talk, I froze up, forgetting what I was saying.

I recovered from this setback by simply stating my speaking goal for the occasion. I told the audience that I have spent a good portion of my life helping to equip people with the knowledge they needed to share their perspectives so that they could feel more confident and make themselves heard. I explained my brief stumble by saying that because of my passion for this topic I'd gotten ahead of myself. Clarity about my goal allowed me to hone my speaking with precision even in this most uncomfortable and unflattering of moments. I acknowledged what everyone in the room had observed—I had stumbled—and then brought everyone's attention back to where it belonged—on the next play.

There is a famous Zen parable that helps us remember not to judge gaffes or victories—our own, or others—too quickly. A farmer learns that his horse has escaped its pen. When his neighbors comment on his bad luck, he says, "Maybe." When his horse returns along with several wild horses, his neighbors remark on this good turn of fortune. "Maybe," the farmer responds again. When his son later tries to ride one of the wild horses and suffers injury upon being thrown off, the neighbors console the farmer. His response: "Maybe." Shortly afterward, the farmer learns that his son's injuries have caused the army to disqualify his son from participating in a military draft. More great news, but yet again the wise farmer responds with, "Maybe."[18]

We can never know how an event or a statement will ultimately impact our lives. Seemingly negative turns of fate can turn out to be blessings in disguise, while apparent windfalls can bring hidden costs. It's best not to spend time dwelling on either positive or negative results and instead stay focused on our larger goal. The next time we experience a setback and feel tempted to ruminate, we can tell ourselves, "Maybe." And then proceed to the next play.

● ● ● TRY IT ● ● ●

Before entering a situation where you might be put on the spot, try writing down "maybe" on a piece of paper and carrying that paper with you in your pocket. The act of writing it down and the feel of it in your pocket might remind you to suspend judgment on what you say or do and simply move on to the next play. Alternatively, you might program your smartphone to send you an alert with the word "maybe" five minutes before an expected spontaneous situation.

Finding the Upside in the Downside

Years ago, when I was leading a team in a corporate setting, my bosses informed me that I would have to lay off around ten people, a quarter of my direct reports. The news came as a tremendous shock. I had never before had to let go of so many people all at once. Although I knew our business had softened due to larger economic forces, my bosses had told me just a week earlier that my team would be exempt from layoffs. Most of my employees were close friends—it would be awful to have to deliver this news to them. I felt besieged in every sense of the word. My self-image as a kind, empathetic person and a support- ive boss was under threat.

I had little choice but to pull myself together and set up meetings with the affected employees. My first meeting was with Sandy, a good friend and senior manager for our East Coast team. As she walked into the conference room, I felt sick to my stomach. I worried about the impact the layoff would have on her, and whether she and I would be able to part on good terms. I worried as well whether I would be able to rise to the occasion and behave as compassionately as possible in this situation.

As I closed the door behind us, an idea occurred to me. Yes, having to let Sandy go was terrible. It would make life difficult for her, and it would also threaten my own sense of self. But what if I could salvage at least something of value in this most unpleasant part of my job? I thought about the different possible ways to frame what was happen- ing. Yes, job loss is always a painful and upsetting experience, but were there any benefits and resources built into the severance packages that might be worth highlighting to help people begin to imagine their next steps? Could I help my employees and friends get beyond panic, as understandable as that was, so that they could start to plan their next steps?

Although Sandy had done a great job in her role, I happened to know that her true passion lay elsewhere. For years, she had talked about wanting to go off and start a mentoring and tutoring program for disadvantaged kids. She had been volunteering for similar programs for a while now and had really enjoyed it. She described her work as a mentor as fulfilling, a refuge, and had repeatedly indicated that she wanted to deepen her involvement and incorporate techniques and practices she had learned from the work we did together.

As we sat down, I told Sandy about the layoff in clear, direct terms. After giving her a few minutes to react, I began to explore with her how the company might support her in finally starting her own mentoring program. Telling her about the package she'd be receiving, we went on to brainstorm other benefits the company was offering and how they might serve her in a new line of work. Building off one another, we tossed around ideas for how she could borrow elements of our own educational efforts at the company in designing her new program.

Our conversation lasted about an hour, and it was painful for her and sad for me. Still, it went better than I had imagined. Sandy didn't leave in a state of despair. Mingled with anger at our company and other negative feelings was a palpable excitement about the future. As hard as it would be to leave her job, she was able to see it as a potential turning point in her career, a chance to build on what she'd been doing and to finally connect with her true passion. During the months that followed, Sandy wound up starting the mentoring program. She went on to do a lot of good.

My epiphany with Sandy informed how I handled subsequent conversations with the other employees on my team. I acknowledged and validated the pain that they were feeling, but I also tried to highlight the opportunity that was at hand. I made sure that I could answer questions about details of their packages and that I knew where to direct them when I lacked information. During most of these conversations, we spent time brainstorming potential future directions for my team members. A number of employees wrote me afterward to thank me for how I'd broken the news to them and handled their departure.

As I now realize, I mobilized each of the four mindset shifts we've discussed in this chapter. By focusing on the layoffs as a potential career turning point, I alerted my team members to how they might position themselves to grow further (growth mindset). Instead of obsessing over how hard these conversations were for me, I steered the discussion back toward my employees and their needs (focus on the audience). As my team members and I went back and forth brainstorming future career possibilities, we were able to validate and build on what one another was saying ("Yes, and . . ."). Instead of allowing myself to get bogged down in my emotional reaction to and disappointment in my own bosses' decision-making, I pushed myself to move on and have what I hoped would be productive conversations with my team members. I also tried to help them refrain from dwelling on what had happened and instead to focus on the futures that could unfold before them (next play).

These conversations with my team members were some of the most difficult I've ever had. I would characterize them as a blend of prepared and spontaneous communication. My bosses had instructed me to transition employees out of the company in specific ways, but I didn't know how these conversations would go and I anticipated that I would have to spend a good deal of time improvising in the moment. By reframing challenges as opportunities, I was able to bring out my best self, to the benefit of my team members. I wasn't in a position to change reality. But I could make it at least a little more tolerable by preparing ahead of time and attending to my audience's needs.

All of us can do the same, not merely in dark moments such as this, but in lighter ones as well. We can focus on the opportunity at hand, freeing ourselves to be more creative, joyous, vibrant—to have more fun. I invite you to make this subtle but important mental shift. Uncurl from your defensive posture. Detach yourself emotionally from the final outcome. Allow yourself to get lost a little and to entertain all that might be possible. In a great many situations, positive and surprising things can happen, but only if we do our part, changing our mindset and approach. By moderating our need for control and protection and adopting a posture of openness, curiosity, and equanimity, we create new space for our authentic personalities to shine. We open the way for learning and growth to take place—our own, and more importantly, that of our audiences.

◉ ◉ ◉ DRILL IT ◉ ◉ ◉

1. Reflect on a recent occasion in which you had to speak spontaneously. What did others learn from you? How did

what you say benefit them? What steps can you take before future impromptu speaking situations to remind yourself of the value you can bring to your audience?

2. During your next spontaneous situation, ask yourself where you and the person with whom you're speaking might agree. Next, ask what might be inhibiting your willingness to agree with this person. By reflecting on your two answers you can become more open to assuming a "Yes, and . . ." posture.

3. Think about an upcoming situation in which you might have to speak spontaneously. Make a list of the biggest opportunities that you think might arise out of it. Do any of them surprise or excite you? Now make a list of the biggest threats you perceive. Do any of these look less scary now that you're also thinking about the opportunities?

Chapter 4: Listen

DON'T JUST DO SOMETHING . . . STAND THERE!

Sometimes the best way to communicate is to say nothing at all.

When most people think about communication, they focus on speaking. But if we're going to be effective in the moment, we also have to *listen*, paying close attention to our audiences' mental and emotional state and using the information we gain to inform what we say.

Fred Dust, author of the book *Making Conversation* and former senior partner and global managing director for the design firm IDEO, has seen the power of listening firsthand.[1] In 2010, he had the privilege of serving as part of a team advising senior members of the Greek government. The government was in big trouble economically and searching for ways to gain infusions of cash. One possibility officials were entertaining was selling a large plot of seaside land that had formerly served as an airport to the government of Qatar, which would develop it. Senior Greek officials, including the prime minister and other cabinet members, held an open meeting with Dust and other experts to publicly solicit their advice on whether the deal was a good idea.

To most of these consultants, Dust included, selling the land seemed like a no-brainer, an easy way to help the country avoid a potential bankruptcy. The land in its present state didn't seem to be adding much value for the country—it was just a derelict former airport strewn with debris. The Qataris were poised to do something interesting and productive with it, benefiting Greece's economy.

The Greek government appeared to agree with this assessment and seemed bent on proceeding with the property's sale. Rather than an open discussion about the deal, organizers of the meeting conceived of it as a scripted affair in which consultants would tell Greek officials that they should sell the land so as to build public support for the plan.

Dust entered the meeting prepared to endorse the deal and offer some thoughts on why it made sense. But as the conversation unfolded, he noticed something interesting. Although Greek officials spoke positively about the deal, some appeared ambivalent. In subtle and less-subtle ways, the officials seemed to acknowledge how important it was that Athenians, as a traditionally oceangoing people, be connected physically with the sea. Since this land was one of the last oceanfront plots near Athens, and since earlier real estate projects elsewhere in the city had served to reduce the public's contact with the waterfront, the implication was that Athens would be losing something culturally and spiritually important if the land were sold. "You could see and feel that this deal was actually quite disturbing to them," Dust said, "the notion of dispensing with the last piece of oceanfront property that Athens had."[2]

When it came Dust's turn to speak, he made a spontaneous decision to scrap what he had prepared and instead articulate the unease about the plan he perceived people were feeling. He didn't tell the Greeks not to do the deal, but he did acknowledge their ambivalence and what they would be sacrificing if it went through. Doing so was risky—the cameras were rolling, and he didn't want to cause problems for his Greek hosts. As he remembers it, he felt uneasy and sick to his stomach as he spoke. But he went with his intuition anyway, telling officials what he felt they needed and wanted to hear.

What happened next startled Dust. As the meeting adjourned, several burly security men surrounded him. Dust thought he had screwed up and the government was escorting him out of the country. But then the prime minister came over to speak with him. "He asked if we could have dinner and said that I had articulated precisely what he and his fellow officials had been feeling." In the end, the Greek government decided not to sell the land to the Qataris. Greek officials would still need to solve the country's fiscal crisis, but at least they could feel satisfied that in this instance they had not betrayed the heritage of their capital city. By staying alert and listening closely to what the Greek politicians were *really* saying, Dust was able to respond authentically on the fly and have a profound—and quite positive—impact on his audience.

We so often miss opportunities during spontaneous encounters to look for signs of what others around us are thinking, feeling, and needing. Often, we miss these opportunities due to noise: physical, physiological, and psychological. The environment might be noisy or distracting—we can barely hear ourselves think, much less attend to what others are thinking or feeling. Our bodies can distract us—we feel nervous, tired, or hungry and have a harder time paying attention. Finally, mental factors can intrude. We judge what we hear or rehearse what we intend to say next. Our own biases or sense of status leads us to overlook others' perspectives and to focus instead on ourselves.

The 3 P's That Impede Us from Listening Well

1. **P**hysical noise
2. **P**hysiological noise (fatigue, hunger, and anxiety)
3. **P**sychological noise (biases, judging, and rehearsing)

The Power of Listening

To truly connect with our audiences, we have established the importance of fighting distraction and orienting ourselves toward them. We must listen to what they're saying and how they are saying it for clues on how we might most effectively connect. By observing our surroundings, we can pay attention not just to the words but to nonverbal and situational signs that evoke their deeper emotions, desires, and needs. How are audience members reacting to what we're saying or doing? How is our current social environment influencing our interaction? What about our communication is resonating—and what isn't? What signals are they sending about how they feel in the moment?

Striving to answer such questions allows us to steer our communications in ways that others find more relevant, thoughtful, and compelling. In turn, we wind up creating new opportunities for ourselves, whether it's a chance to build trust, forge a new relationship, connect more powerfully in the moment, appreciate others' perspectives better, or just operate more effectively.

Learning to listen allows us to uncover previously unknown information or insights. It allows us to recognize patterns sooner and in different ways. Ari Fleischer, White House press secretary under President George W. Bush, called this listening via "osmosis." He describes how he was able to do his job better when he was staying alert and absorbing information rather than merely giving it out. He learned early that he could never hope to serve as the expert in every room he was in, given the vast array of topics and policies he encountered throughout the day. Rather than beating himself up over situations in which he felt underprepared, Fleischer began to focus on soaking in the verbal and nonverbal information. Coming across new information about a policy area like Social Security or defense, he would make a mental note and store this information. He could make use of it later at opportune times—when asking a follow-up question, say, or when articulating an opinion. In effect, he would recognize a pattern, connecting something he'd seen earlier with something else that he was now seeing or hearing. "Osmosis really worked," he says. "It's amazing how much you absorb. It's a myriad of issues a press secretary gets exposed to, and you better [absorb it all]. That way, when it comes up in the briefing room, you can address it."[3]

My improv mentor Adam Tobin tells a story about a time he was pitching a new television show concept to a studio vice president. One of the first questions the vice president asked him was why his show wasn't "a sci-fi story." It was an odd query that seemed to come out of nowhere—Tobin had never thought of the show he was pitching as science fiction. Yet he didn't brush off the question as silly or move on from it. Leveraging his skills as an expert listener and improviser, Tobin leaned in, inquiring why the assistant had asked the question.

The vice president told Tobin that he had asked not so much because Tobin's show idea seemed like science fiction but because his boss was nervous about producing anything that smacked of science fiction—his last three ventures in that genre had failed. "What this person was doing," Tobin reflects, "was actually asking me for ammunition that he could then take to his boss to sell my story. He was solving a problem that I didn't even know existed."[4] By taking time to listen and be present, Tobin gleaned new information that would allow him to communicate more successfully in this current pitching situation as well as in the future. He enhanced the degree of opportunity open to him through careful listening.

Listening also opens up opportunities by helping us connect to those around us. One research study grouped participants in pairs, with one person listening and the other speaking. Some of the listeners received text messages while the speakers were talking—a deliberate attempt by the researchers to distract them. Those speakers whose listeners weren't visibly distracted were sharper, less anxious, and more eager to share their thoughts. The more we listen, the more headway we're liable to make with others. In subsequent studies with employees, researchers found that "listening seems to make an employee more relaxed, more self-aware of his or her strengths and weaknesses, and more willing to reflect in a nondefensive manner."[5] By allowing more information to flow and making collaboration easier, we can create more opportunity for connection and increase the chances that our spontaneous speaking will land successfully with our audience.

Conversely, by failing to listen, we miss out on opportunities and sometimes even create new problems, communicating in ways that strike our audiences as jarring, tone-deaf, or off-putting. When I was in my early twenties, I interned for a famous film director and producer. On one occasion, I attended a meeting my boss was holding with several important Japanese film executives. I was familiar with Japanese cultural norms, so I knew that business professionals from Japan tend to present business cards in a more formal way than Americans typically do. When you first meet a business contact in Japan, you hold one of your cards in both hands, gaze down at it, and then hand it to the other person. The receiver of the card likewise takes great care, accepting the card in both hands, gazing at it, and then placing it on the table in front of them.[6]

My boss was oblivious to this ritual. When several of his guests handed him their cards, he did what most Americans would do: collect them into a stack, put them unceremoniously in his wallet, and then sit down to start the meeting. Mistakes like this happen all the time in business, but we usually can salvage the situation if we stay alert to people's responses. My boss didn't do that. He failed to pick up subtle and not-so-subtle signs that he'd committed a faux pas—a stiffening in the shoulders of his guests, a nervous smile, an awkward silence. Two guests sitting just feet away from him exchanged confused and disapproving glances. Even a novice like me could see that something inappropriate had just happened. The meeting continued for another hour and the tension in the air never dissipated, but my boss didn't seem to notice.

We've all failed to listen during spontaneous encounters and paid the price. Perhaps we've thrown our support behind an idea before taking the time to find out if the team thinks it's the optimal solution. Perhaps we've rushed to offer a solution to a problem articulated by our significant other, when in fact all they want is to vent and feel heard. Perhaps we've asked someone out on a date because they seem to like us, when in fact they were only trying to be friendly. We could avoid so many of the small—and not-so-small—miscues that arise in daily life if we simply paid more attention to what others are truly communicating to us.

Becoming More Attentive

How might we listen better in the midst of a spontaneous speaking situation? Drawing on his experiences playing college basketball, Stanford lecturer and consultant Collins Dobbs has created a useful three-step framework for handling difficult encounters with others called Pace, Space, and Grace.[7] We can use this framework to orient ourselves toward listening not just during challenging conversations, but in any interaction we have with others. In essence, the framework prompts us to slow down just a bit, reflect on what might be going on in the minds of others around us, and cue into *our* intuitive sense of what's happening. The end result is more empathic listening and better, more informed communication in the moment. Let's look, learn, and listen.

Step #1—Slow Your Pace

Life comes at us fast, and as a result, so many of us end up thinking fast, speaking fast, and listening fast. By slowing down and focusing on simply being present and paying attention, we can become more receptive to messages from others we might otherwise miss.

Former NPR journalist Debra Schifrin has a technique she uses when interviewing others called the "killer last question." As an interview is wrapping up, she'll ask her interviewee if there is anything important that she neglected to ask. Sometimes the person responds immediately, but if they don't, she does something radical. She waits. And waits some more. Most of the time, they respond that her questions covered everything. But Schifrin waits for a bit longer, letting the seconds tick by. "And then," she relates, "they will say the most interesting thing that they said in the whole interview."[8]

Schifrin theorizes that the dead time liberates interviewees because she in effect is giving them control over the conversation. This "creates a condition where they're more likely to share something, or at the end of this conversation, we've been talking about a lot of things, it lets them ask a question of themselves and get to an answer" that excites them.

Shifrin's killer last question exemplifies the first strategy we can deploy to listen better in the moment. As Schifrin's example suggests, slowing our pace can also demonstrate interest and respect on our part.

There are many actions we can take to slow our pace—not just at the end of the conversation, but at any time. We can put away our phones when sitting across the table from someone. We can take deep breaths. We can repeat mantras to ourselves, something like "I'm here for you" or "This is important, so I should pay attention." We can remind ourselves of how important it is to listen.

● ● ● **TRY IT** ● ● ●

Practice pausing during your communication with others. To become more comfortable with this tactic, experiment with it first in conversations that are low stakes or conversational.

Slowing down isn't only about making more time. It's also about what we *do* with that time. We must listen *actively*, quieting our minds and reducing judgment so that we can better understand the gist of what others are saying, and so that others can perceive that we're paying attention. Academic experts have likened listening to a "muscle" that "requires training, persistence, effort, and most importantly, the intention to become a good listener."[9] To listen more intently, we can take steps like maintaining eye contact, conveying to others that we're listening via our facial expressions or head nodding, reflecting on what we're hearing, asking open-ended questions, and so on.[10] We can also avoid holding conversations when we're distracted, rescheduling them for times when we know we can really focus.

Honing our listening abilities often means attending to the nuances of our own and others' nonverbal communication. Guy Itzchakov, a well-known listening expert who teaches at the University of Haifa, told me how a couples counselor he knows stays alert to the dynamics that unfold thanks to subtle cues their clients give during sessions. Often, when one member of a couple (usually the male) becomes uncomfortable, he'll point his feet toward the door, as if he wants to leave. Although he might not express discomfort explicitly, his partner notices this cue either consciously or not, and it puts them on the defensive. They in turn will tighten up—they'll cross their arms, take a step back, or hunch their shoulders to make themselves small. We must stay alert for behavioral cues into how others are feeling, and we must also notice our own cues that might inhibit others from expressing themselves.[11]

As Itzchakov further notes, we often take shortcuts when confronted by nonverbal communication. We assume we know what a particular gesture means, when in fact these might be highly individualized. "Give the other person more time to speak," Itzchakov advises. "Don't be afraid of silence. People need time to think deeply." When we take time to listen, we can begin to parse the nuances of each person's nonverbal communication. We might find that a speaker's true emotions are somewhat different than what we initially inferred.

Our mindset when listening matters, too. If you're like me, you sometimes react in spontaneous situations by trying to solve a problem that crops up in the course of conversation. You think you're listening, but your problem-solving mindset leads you not to stay silent but instead to interject with a solution. By contrast, "a person with a listening attitude believes that the solution to the speaker's problem lies within the speaker," Itzchakov says. Instead of rushing to offer a solution, someone with a listening mindset might instead try to help the speaker bring out a solution themselves by posing questions, listening closely to their responses, and asking follow-up questions. Questions might include, "Have you encountered a problem like this before?" and "What resources have you used to help you deal with something like this in the past?" When we consciously adopt a listening mindset, people perceive us as better listeners. Much of the time, we probably are.

Slowing our pace to practice active listening can help us to function better in a whole range of spontaneous situations. If we're at a business dinner, we can understand the real reason our manager just asked us to introduce the visiting colleague. If we're in the hallway chatting with our coworker, we can uncover her true motivation when she asks us for feedback. If we're at a party flirting with an attractive somebody, we can learn what this person really likes on a date or the kind of relationship they really want. In all of these spontaneous situations, slowing down can help to build relationships and foster ongoing communication by conveying that we take keen interest in what the other person is saying. We also gain critical reconnaissance that helps us respond in the moment.

● ● ● TRY IT ● ● ●

Watch a video where someone is communicating, and turn the sound down. Notice the person's nonverbal behavior. What are their eyes doing? Are they expansive in their gestures or is their body tightened? How is their body oriented? All of these cues and clues serve either to reinforce or betray what they're trying to convey.

Step #2—Make Space for Reflection
When veteran Silicon Valley designer Bob Baxley presents his work to other executives, he doesn't spend all of his time talking. He makes a

point to listen—a lot. "I never try to respond to feedback in the moment and redesign the thing in real time," he says. "I coach my team to do the same thing. This is our moment to just listen and take notes. We'll synthesize later what we hear and try to make sense of it."[12] Fred Dust takes a similar approach. When something he hears triggers a response in him that might take him off in a new direction, he restrains himself so that he has time to think. "You shouldn't feel like you should be forced into having to respond," he says.

In addition to moderating our pace, we can listen better in the moment by carving out space for ourselves to reflect on what we've heard. We've taken the time to open ourselves up to others' perspectives. Now we must ponder our own responses and how we might best meet the other person's needs.

One step we can take to buy ourselves time and gain the space we need to make sense of signals we're receiving from others is to ask clarifying questions: What makes you believe this? How does this help? What more can you tell me? As Schifrin observes, the act of posing a question requires a certain amount of bravery on our part. We're relinquishing control to the other person by inviting them to respond, and we might feel nervous about where the conversation might lead. Yet, doing so can allow us to process what we hear, while again sending cues that we are paying attention, helping us to gain further details and insights.

● ● ● TRY IT ● ● ●

Over the next day, make a point of asking several clarifying questions in the course of three conversations in which you're a part. Make it your mission to get the other person to explain to you the problem they are trying to solve, the feelings they hope to share, or the information they need. Notice how you get more detail and how you feel less pressure to respond right away.

I know how difficult—but also how helpful—it can be to pose clarifying questions. Not long ago, while I was teaching communication skills to a group of seventy-five start-up founders and executives, one of them approached me during a break to offer unsolicited feedback about my presentation. This gentleman disliked my material and how I was presenting it. He accused me of "being wrong" and "teaching people to be boring."

My first inclination was to react defensively or politely brush this person off. Instead, I tried to create some space to understand what exactly he was saying. I asked him to "help me understand why this is teaching people to be boring."

As painful as it was to hear this audience member out, I did it. Processing what he was saying, I realized that he wasn't having a bad day or trying to be a jerk—he was well-intentioned and genuinely wanted to see me succeed. This new awareness on my part shifted the meaning of his remarks—I was now willing to take them more seriously. His biggest concern had to do with the sequencing of my material. While I was trying to scaffold knowledge in a logical and methodical manner, he felt my buildup was too slow and disengaging. His feedback helped me, and I never would have heard it had I not allowed myself space to reflect on his initial feedback. Further, the time I gained while he was answering my questions allowed me to respond more appropriately. When I deliver the content he deemed "boring," I now set it up by posing a question that gets my audiences engaged up front and interested in seeing where I am going to take them.

Beyond asking clarifying questions, a second way we might create an opening for reflection is to paraphrase what we've just heard a speaker say. Paraphrasing isn't parroting back what the other person said (for example, "What I hear you saying is . . ."). Rather, it's distilling the essence of what we heard them communicate. Doing so can serve a number of purposes depending on the context: It can ensure that we understood someone's meaning correctly. It can allow us to acknowledge an emotion that someone is feeling. It can give us a chance to make connections between ideas. It can show others that we've been listening. And in most situations, it can also allow us to step back and think about what we've been hearing.

Adam Tobin notes that paraphrasing serves in effect to extend the present moment for just a little bit longer. By articulating your sense of what someone just said, "you're kind of . . . living in that space for a little moment. . . . It's like, 'Okay, before we rush on to what we think about that or what that means, like let's take a moment and just be in that for a sec.'"[13] Giving ourselves some space allows us to get our bearing rather than allowing a conversation to rush past us.

Several years back, I was invited to facilitate a strategic planning initiative at a community college where I taught. Time was of the essence, and the conversation sometimes got heated. I often found myself paraphrasing monologues or longer group discussions with short statements like "Cost sounds important" or "The implementation time must be considered." My paraphrasing not only focused the topics being discussed; it allowed for some space and time for myself and the participants to reflect and consider our next actions.

Both questions and paraphrasing focus on what others around us have said. A final way to make space focuses on what went *unsaid.* We can remark on what we just heard and clarify the speaker's meaning by asking about something they omitted. This tactic works well when someone offers you a suggestion or spontaneous critical feedback. In pointing out an opportunity for you or a mistake you made, they might describe the consequences for their team. You could say, "I'm hearing that cost and timing must be considered jointly. I hadn't considered the interaction of those two factors. How does this impact your team and you?" Asking for elaboration in this way can help you unearth and reflect on powerful feelings the speaker is experiencing that might be lingering beneath the surface. As you come to understand these feelings, you might well have a clearer idea of how to respond in a way that is productive and helpful.

Here is another way to use this "what I didn't hear" question to keep a conversation moving. Students I teach or people I coach often experience high levels of speaking anxiety. They will share their challenges, fears, and issues. I try to validate what I hear, but my first observation in most cases is, "While I understand fully how speaking is often nerve-racking for you, can you talk about the times you successfully spoke and weren't as nervous." Not only does this question help the folks I work with to realize that they are not always nervous; it gives me space to reflect on what they have said so that I can better respond in the moment.

Some Key Ways to Give Yourself Space

• Ask clarifying questions.
• Paraphrase what you hear.
• Comment on what *hasn't* been said.

Step #3—Grace

Some years ago, my friend John's beloved French grandmother passed away. His *grand-mère*, as he called her, had played a pivotal role in his life, and he wanted to do something special to honor her and express his grief. When his mother told him that a relatively new parish priest who barely knew *grand-mère* would deliver the eulogy at her funeral, John asked if he might do it instead. He felt his *grand-mère* deserved to have someone who loved her speak about her life, not a stranger.

For two days leading up to the funeral, John wrote and rewrote his eulogy, trying to craft his remarks and get them just right. The right anecdotes. The right tone. The right structure. The right length. The right language. When he felt satisfied that he was communicating exactly what he felt in his heart and what his audience might appreciate, he jotted the final speech down on note cards word for word. He had given a few speeches as a high school student, reading them in front of crowds of fellow students. He felt fairly confident that his skills as a communicator would see him through. Still, he felt anxious, wondering whether he'd be able to perform well amid his grief and in the formal environment of a church chapel, with the priest and others in the community looking on.

At his *grand-mère*'s funeral, John felt butterflies in his stomach as the priest called his name, inviting him to deliver the eulogy. More than a hundred people sat in the pews, including many John didn't know. As he walked up to the pulpit, he did the best he could to keep himself from breaking down. When he reached the lectern, however, another, bigger problem presented itself. He felt in his suit pocket for the cards, and they weren't there. He felt around again, his heart pounding, the breath catching in his throat. Nothing.

A hundred faces stared up at him, waiting for him to begin. "For a moment there," John recalls, "I felt like running off the altar." But he didn't. Gazing out at his extended family and seeing their expressions of grief and sadness, he remembered why he had come—to commemorate and celebrate his *grand-mère*'s life—and decided to improvise. After all, he thought, "Everything I had written on my note cards was already inscribed in my heart." Maybe he could still convey the essence of what he'd wanted to say.

John proceeded as best he could, interspersing memories he recalled from his prepared eulogy with new ones that came to him in the moment, adding some quick reflections he thought of as he gauged the audience's reaction. At one point, when audience members seemed to shift in their seats, he realized he was veering off too far on a tangent and gave himself a moment to pick a new direction. At another, as he saw tears on the face of a family member, his own throat caught with emotion. Given the circumstances, he reminded himself that this was completely understandable. Each time, he managed to recover and get back on track, and it was okay. "I am sure my words were not perfect, but the feelings I expressed were one hundred percent authentic. Instead of looking at my scribbles as I spoke, I got to see the faces of other loved ones, marked with tears and smiles."

Thrust unexpectedly into a spontaneous communication situation, John made the most of it by listening. He registered the emotions of others in attendance and remained sensitive to his internal voice, which told him not to run but instead to put his trust in himself and to wing it. He continued to pay attention to his internal voice as he delivered his remarks, processing the reactions of those around him and letting his internal voice guide his behavior in response.

As soon as John stepped down from the altar, he knew that his eulogy was well received. Some of his relatives shot him grateful looks. His mother and sisters reached over and hugged him or grasped his hand as he sat down. Because his words were spontaneous and not rigidly planned, and because he had attended to others' emotions as well as to his own internal voice in delivering his remarks, his eulogy came across as more authentic and meaningful, even if it wasn't perfect—in fact, *because* it wasn't.

In the context of spontaneous encounters, listening presents us with a paradox. Doing it well doesn't just involve paying close attention to others. It also means cuing in to the small voices inside our own heads, the inner dialogue that ticks on as we're communicating with others. Interpersonal relationships experts David Bradford and Carole Robin note that to connect well with others we must "pick up two signals from two different antennas," one internal and the other external.[14] They suggest that whenever we are in conversation with someone, there are two dialogues going on: the one we are having with the other person(s) and the one we are having with ourselves. We need to respect both of these.

So often we presume we must focus exclusively on others when we listen to them, and that if we don't, we're somehow bad listeners. We're supposed to cancel out or dampen our own feelings and judgments as they arise, pretending that they don't exist. We do better in spontaneous situations if we show ourselves a little grace and give ourselves permission to have our inner voice heard as well. Of course, we shouldn't let our feelings and judgments overwhelm what we hear from others, but we shouldn't ignore or discount them entirely, either.

Drawing on our past experience, we should validate our feelings, even in cases when we're not particularly proud of them. To the extent we can, we should scrutinize our feelings, noticing patterns and pondering why we're feeling and thinking as we are. When our internal voice strikes us as particularly compelling, we should pay attention and potentially take action. Quite often in conversations, we'll hear ourselves say "That doesn't feel right" or "There's something more going on here." In response, we can decide to follow up with actions such as asking more questions, rethinking our initial responses, or ending the conversation. Showing grace for ourselves means allowing room for introspection and then on a minute-by-minute basis allowing our introspection to shape our behavior.

Look consciously for opportunities to convey emotions that you might be feeling in the course of interacting with others. Challenge yourself during your next three substantive conversations to interject at least once or twice, expressing emotions you're feeling. You might say something like, "You know, what you're saying brings an interesting feeling up for me . . ." and then elaborate as best you can. Externalizing your emotions can get you in the habit of registering your internal voice more strongly and listening to it. In so doing, you're training yourself to feel and share more.

Listening for What Needs to Be Done—and Doing It

At a TED conference in 2008, a panel discussion being filmed by the BBC was under way when the proceedings halted due to a technical problem. Awkwardness ensued as the host, a BBC on-air personality, struggled to fill in the dead time. Then someone in the audience spoke up, seemingly out of nowhere—an apparent heckler. According to one eyewitness, he "began speaking loudly as if he were conducting a live news feed, joking that he was reporting live from TED but 'couldn't understand a [expletive] word' and was 'wondering why at a technology conference everything is running so shittily.'"[15]

It was none other than the comic legend Robin Williams, eager and willing to salvage the event, probably to the great interest and relief of its organizers.

Williams sauntered onstage for some impromptu banter, tossing out rapid-fire jokes on diverse subjects including the physicist Stephen Hawking, Google, the country of Israel, and the British royal family. Williams's off-the-cuff musings were so funny that the event's organizer came onstage and asked if he'd come back the following day to say a few words.

Encountering an unexpected situation, Williams stepped into the fray, doing what needed to be done to keep the audience happy and fill the time while the technicians figured out how to solve the problem. How did he pull it off? Clearly, he was a comedic genius who was unafraid to reveal his personality in a public setting. But he also deployed skills available to any of us. When the glitch occurred, he was present and paying attention. Not only did he realize that an opportunity existed to step up—he tuned in to the emotions and perceptions of his fellow audience members and delivered jokes that in some way captured or played off them. He was clearly cuing in to the needs and desires of others around him.

We are all capable of doing the same. We can communicate fairly well in impromptu situations if we take the lessons of previous chapters to heart, learning to control our anxiety, restraining our drive toward perfectionism, and seeing spontaneous moments as opportunities rather than threats. But we can't truly connect with others unless we pay attention to them as well as to ourselves, creating an ongoing dialogue in our minds between what we're picking up from others and what our own, internal voices are saying we should do in response. We can't create, experience, and project that kind of pitch-perfect communication Williams spawned that day unless we're listening, in the fullest sense of the word. That means adding more pace, space, and grace to our spontaneous communication.

● ● ● DRILL IT ● ● ●

1. Now that you've experimented with asking clarifying questions to create space for listening, prepare some of these questions in advance. Examples might be, "Can you provide more specific detail?" "Can you share with me some of your experiences with this?" "How does this apply to what you're currently working on?" "How can this help you and others?" Having questions ready can alleviate pressure you might feel in the moment.

2. To practice paraphrasing, listen to other people speaking live in person or perhaps on a podcast or other interviews and think to yourself, "The bottom line here is . . ." Do this over and over to habituate yourself to distilling key points. If possible, you might also wish on occasion to confirm with the speaker whether your paraphrase of their communication was accurate.

3. Take a few minutes to ask a trusted other about your recent listening. How strong a listener do they think you are? Do you tend to listen better or worse at certain times or in

certain contexts? Do certain subjects cause your attention to drift or prompt you to interject a comment too quickly? Do disconnects between what they think they're saying and what you hear frequently arise? If listening is in fact a problem in your relationship, see if this other person would be willing to check in with you periodically to give additional feedback.

Chapter 5: Structure

STRUCTURE YOUR SPONTANEITY

*When you're speaking spontaneously, having a road map
doesn't bog you down. It frees you up.*

We all have our quirky talents. Some of us can curl our tongues.
Others can ride on a unicycle without falling. I have an uncanny
ability to walk backward in a straight line as I carry on a lively conversation. I developed this talent while working as a campus tour guide
in college. I was desperate for money, and it was the highest-paying
job I could find. Day after day, I led groups of parents and prospective
students around the Stanford University campus, pointing out important sights while edging backward without stumbling or crashing into
anything.

My skill as a backward-walking conversationalist is of limited use
today (especially since so much of our communication is now virtual). But working as a tour guide served me well in another respect.
I learned many lessons, perhaps none more valuable than the importance of structure in communication. The number one rule my supervisors drilled into me during my three months of training was *never
lose your tour group.* To ensure that I didn't, my bosses trained me to set
expectations well and to provide visitors with a clear path or direction.
In other words, they taught me to give tours in a structured way.

The lessons I learned about how to be a great tour guide can help
you change the way you think about preparing for a big conversation.
Yes, you read that right: we can in fact prepare for impromptu communication. So far in this book, I've talked about how to get comfortable

speaking spontaneously and being present in the moment to respond to your audience. But we can also take certain steps in advance—not to pre-script an interaction or memorize what we'll say, but simply to create some boundaries and habits for ourselves that increase the odds that we'll communicate well on the fly. One of the most important steps we can take is to think about structure and how we design our messages.

When I started my tours, I didn't simply say, "Hi, I'm Matt. Let's go," and start sharing whatever information struck my fancy. Rather, I started our discussion by outlining for visitors a sense of where we would go, and by extension, where we wouldn't be going. In the process, I answered common questions that many visitors might often have, such as how long the tour would take and whether we would be taking any breaks along the way.

By sketching out a basic road map at the outset and by then executing on that plan, I made it easier for visitors not merely to stay with me but also to relax, pay attention, and absorb what I was saying. If visitors hadn't known what to expect, a little voice in their minds might have continued to wonder about what they would later experience. Setting expectations at the beginning of the tour made it easier for both me and my audience to pay attention to the details.

When conveying our ideas to others in a wide variety of contexts, we do so much better if we follow a road map or structure and articulate it in some way at the outset. Just like on a tour, this alerts our audience members in advance to what is coming. Think back to the last time you listened to someone ramble when they spoke or meander when they wrote. How did it feel for you? Were you engaged? Was their message clear? Or did you quickly lose patience, get distracted, or tune out?

Many people can appreciate that structure helps with formal presentations. Since we have time to plan our remarks, it makes sense to ensure that our ideas unfold in a logical way. Spontaneous communication seems like a different beast. When someone puts us on the spot and asks us to speak, it's often all that we can do to keep our cool, take stock of the emotional and mental states of those around us, and think of something to say that won't embarrass us. We're improvising, flying by the seat of our pants, so how can we possibly apply a structure to what we want to say, setting expectations so that others around us can follow along? More to the point, why would we even want to? The impulse to impose a structure would seem to take us out of the present moment, rendering our responses to others less fluid and effective.

Structure doesn't impede spontaneous communication—it enables it. When the best jazz musicians improvise, they're not just playing whatever random notes pop into their minds. They're improvising within the bounds of informal, preset musical structures. Jazz musicians typically learn a canon of standard songs, the melody and chord progressions of which serve as structures for improvisation. Knowing a given song structure in advance, musicians can improvise in ways that will sound good over a song's basic chords and possibly reference the melody. The existence of a preordained structure makes it much easier for jazz musicians to compose spontaneously—they have some basic parameters or rules within which to work, and they can use these as a jumping-off point to create something original and of the moment. Song structure also helps orient listeners, giving them a logic that they can follow and preventing jazz from sounding like a muddled mess.

A similar dynamic informs how children play. As playground designer Meghan Talarowski relates, kids need freedom when playing, but they also need a certain amount of structure. "If you just have a blank slate," she says, kids tend to play more violently with one another. They "have a tendency to treat each other like playthings because there's nothing to activate their imagination, nothing for them to riff off of." In designing playgrounds, Talarowski strives to create a basic "frame or stage for good play," one in which kids still have a great deal of latitude to invent and explore spontaneously. Such a frame might take the form of specific play equipment, such as an open-ended net structure that allows kids to move quickly and in ways that they choose, or slides that allow children to improvise how they descend.[1] It might also entail a logical ordering or arrangement of play elements, so that kids make new discoveries and experience a sense of surprise as they move across a playground.

To render structure easier for us, we can follow the example of jazz musicians and arm ourselves in advance with a few versatile and simple road maps that can help us in everyday situations, without going too far and trying to script a spontaneous encounter. That way, when a spontaneous encounter presents itself, we can mobilize a relevant structure and use it almost effortlessly to enhance our power as communicators.

Note to Self: A List Isn't a Structure

When I mention structure to clients and audience members, some of them confuse it with a mere listing of information. They think that if they organize what they want to say into a series of bullet points or slides, they have a structure.

Don't get me wrong: the list can be a wonderful thing. When you're headed to the grocery store or determining who has been naughty or nice, a list can get the job done. But when it comes to communicating spontaneously, lists don't rise to the level of a full-fledged structure. They won't help us respond better and deliver more compelling messages. They're just lists.

A structure as I define it is *a narrative or story that logically connects ideas with one another*, organizing them into a *beginning*, a *middle*, and an *end*. If you rely on a list of bullet points in a spontaneous situation, you've missed the point. Sue Stanley, senior instructional designer at Toastmasters International, agrees. "Structure is an important tenet of any successful speech," she says, "whether it's impromptu or not. You have to be able to get a beginning, a middle, and an end. You have to know where you're going to start and where you're going to end."[2]

When you think about structure as a logical, narrative progression of elements, you start to see it everywhere. Most popular music unfolds according to one of a relatively small number of common structures. One familiar structure, known as ABABCB, begins with an introductory verse (A), continues to the song's chorus (B), goes back to present another verse (A), returns with the chorus (B), and moves to a bridge or transitional section (C) before returning to the chorus and ending (B). Hit songs by artists like Tina Turner, Radiohead, and Katy Perry all follow this structure, which again unfolds logically, offering a clear beginning, middle, and end.[3]

Movies, novels, and other literary works likewise follow common structures. For instance, a common formula in Western literary works is ABDCE: You start by depicting an action (A), continue by providing backstory (B), develop the tension between the characters (D), increase the tension until you reach a climactic moment (C), and then resolve the plot in an ending (E). When you consume a story with a structure like this, the events don't feel like they come at you out of nowhere. They seem to unfold logically.[4]

Legal arguments often unfold according to a structure called IRAC. First you discuss the issue at hand (I), then you present the relevant legal rule that might apply (R), next you present an analysis in which you apply the rule to the issue (A), and finally you come to a conclusion (C). Salespeople often follow a structure called *Problem–Solution–Benefit* when pitching their wares. First, you point to a problem or pain point that is out there in the world and that affects the audience. Next, introduce your product or service and discuss how it solves the problem. Finally, describe the larger benefits customers will gain if they buy the product or service. The next time you watch television commercials, pay attention to the flow of ideas. Chances are, you'll see *Problem–Solution–Benefit* in action. We will discuss this structure in more detail in the second part of the book.

As a seminary student once told me, many sermons display a structure called Me, We, Thee, We, Me. You describe an issue with which you're wrestling (Me), generalize by showing how all of us can relate to this issue (We), invoke wisdom from a deity or holy text that might bear on the issue (Thee), ask the audience to take action in line with the holy teaching (We), and end by explaining how this action or teaching plays out in each individual's life, resolving the initial issue or challenge (Me).

● ● ● **TRY IT** ● ● ●

Take a few minutes to think about your favorite book or popular song and how it flows. Can you identify the underlying structure? Bonus points: listen to a TED Talk or two and see if you can identify the road map the speaker is using.

Keep Them Listening

Why are narratives so useful and powerful when communicating? As a speaker and speaking coach, I've found that structuring my presentation affords at least *four benefits*.

First, as I've suggested, arranging information as a logical story helps *keep our audience's attention and interest*. Beyond previewing where content is going, a story structure has built into it the ability to make connections or transitions between ideas. "There's something propelling a story," historian of education David Labaree remarks. "There's a line of interest that draws you in. It's more of an intellectual struggle to simply follow a logical argument. But if you can weave it together into something that feels like a story, then you're more likely to be able to draw people in."[5]

As a tour guide, I found that if I didn't connect where our group had been to where we were going next, tour members would get lost. They would wander off, either because they felt curious about something they saw and wanted to linger with it, they couldn't grasp the relevance of what they were seeing and their attention drifted, or they worried about what was coming next and thus couldn't focus as well. Something similar holds with impromptu speaking. Without clear bridges between ideas, we'll lose our audiences and they'll go to their phone, their friends, or to sleep.

Someone using words like "next" and "so" when shifting between ideas likely hasn't created a clear enough narrative to hold together the pieces of information they want to share in a logical way. Following a structure pushes us to make connections between ideas explicit, often with a single sentence. The *Problem–Solution–Benefit* structure, for instance, invites a transition like, "Now that we have a firm understanding of the problem at hand, allow me to share how we can solve it through a simple investment"; or "Once we invest in and build out this solution, we will be able to reduce costs and save time."

The best, most robust transitions tend to review what was said and then signpost what is coming next. And they do it in the context of a larger logical flow that we've established at the outset. Note that we don't always have to be perfectly explicit about our overarching structure when beginning impromptu remarks. We can take a subtler approach and still reap the benefits of structure. Rev. Martin Luther King Jr.'s famous "I Have a Dream" speech, which many argue was mostly delivered spontaneously, follows the *Problem–Solution–Benefit* formula. But he never openly calls that out for his audience. Using analogies and other rhetorical devices, he deftly moves from one element to the next, gracefully developing a logical flow.

In general, it's a good idea to give your audience some kind of road map at the outset of a speech of any length, spontaneous or not. Thinking about what you want to communicate in the context of a story structure can be a useful way to organize your thoughts, even when speaking on the spot.

Enhance "Stickiness"

A second way structure helps with spontaneous speaking is by *helping both us and our audience to remember important messages.* We humans are miserable at remembering information. We can barely hold more than seven distinct numbers in our heads at once, and we're probably worse when it comes to remembering complex concepts. Our brains are designed to forget much of what we experience, filtering it out so that we can remember the important stuff. Forgetting "may be the default mode of the brain," one journalist has written.[6] We tend to remember the essence or gist of events, letting go of the details—what scientists somewhat colorfully call "fade to gist."[7]

Yet our brains were also designed to seek out, enjoy, create, and remember structured narratives or stories. In fact, scientists often call our ability to recall long-ago events "episodic" memory because we tend to retain information as episodes or stories. As neuroscientist David Eagleman relates, "[S]tories are crafted to plug into what matters to the brain." In describing just how potent stories are, Eagleman alludes to the scene at the end of the original *Star Wars* movie when Luke Skywalker has to drop a bomb into a tiny, interior hole in the massive Death Star to blow it up. "That's what storytelling is to our brains," he says. "It is the porthole that completely can sway us, can make us feel like 'oh,' make us laugh, make us cry, make us understand someone else's point of view, or at least push in that direction. So that is really at the heart of what neuroscience tells us about how to, how we communicate and how we engage people."[8]

By structuring our communication as a logical sequence with a beginning, middle, and end, we prime our messages to be noticed and remembered, both by ourselves and our audiences. One study of students giving in-class presentations found that only a few told stories, but that their peers found these stories far more memorable than statistics. Queried afterward, 63 percent of students reported recalling stories from the presentations while only 5 percent recalled data points.[9]

Stories enable us to connect with audiences not only on the level of abstract reason or logic but also emotion, which in turn might well help us remember information better. Stanford neurologist Frank Longo, reflecting on the neurological basis for narrative's power, speculates that "if my story can elicit some emotion in you, besides remembering it better, you just might find it more interesting. Emotion can rev up the circuits in the brain devoted to paying attention. So if I'm an effective storyteller, I'm figuring out how to arouse your attention circuits, your memory circuits, and part of that could be through the emotional component."[10] Unlike a mere list, storytelling can even potentially transform our audiences through the emotional connections it forges—changing their minds, soothing or invigorating their souls, inspiring them to take action.[11] As behavioral scientist Jennifer Aaker reflects, "Those who tell the best stories will become the best leaders," precisely because they activate both the rational and emotional parts of audience members' brains.[12]

By aiding memory, structure can also allow our communication to spread. As a veteran communications consultant to well-known clients in the tech industry, Raymond Nasr often helps entrepreneurs prepare for high-stakes meetings with venture capitalists in which they attempt to secure funding for their firms. In these meetings, entrepreneurs usually must present their own personal histories and those of their start-up ventures. Rather than deliver this background as a series of disconnected facts, Nasr counsels them to structure their accounts as narratives with a clear beginning, middle, and end. Their stories, he argues, should emphasize a strong sense of tension driving events forward, and they should end in a catharsis that delivers a feeling of resolution.

As Nasr explains, one of the greatest benefits of adopting a narrative structure is "repeatability." Often, the venture capitalist with whom an entrepreneur might be meeting isn't the one making the final decision about whether to provide funding. That person has to go back to their firm and pitch the entrepreneur's company to others. If entrepreneurs tell a well-crafted story, it will more likely stick with those hearing it, and they in turn will have an easier time repeating it so that it sticks with their listeners. Over time, Nasr reflects, the repeatability of a story among listeners "changes a mere narrative into mythology. Because it gets repeated generation upon generation upon generation."[13]

The best stories don't simply impart information. They make it meaningful, enlightening, and energizing. In the process, a simple communication takes on a life of its own. Who wouldn't want this kind of impact for their spontaneous speaking? I know I would.

● ● ● TRY IT ● ● ●

The next time you need to convince someone to do or think something, try taking Nasr's advice and structuring what you intend to say as a narrative with a clear beginning, middle, and end. You might try this at work when trying to convince your boss and coworkers to take a certain course of action or at home to get your unruly teenager to change their behavior. Telling a story that begins with a clear problem, raises the stakes with tension in the middle, and then resolves with a memorable ending will help illustrate the point you want to make in a way that is hard to ignore or forget.

Make It Easier for Your Audience

Structure's third benefit—in addition to helping people engage with our communication more fully and remember it better—is that it *makes processing information easier*. In part, this is because we explicitly signal the structure to readers and help them orient themselves as they receive information. In researching this book, I spoke with Myka Carroll, editorial director of the For Dummies brand and author of *New York City for Dummies*.[14] As she relates, the popular For Dummies franchise follows a very clear format that contains cues and guideposts for readers. The franchise's objective is to assist readers with a process called "way finding," a term borrowed from hiking or adventuring that "is also applicable to the information-seeking experience, where we are also trying to 'orient' ourselves in relation to what we do and don't know in a learning journey."[15] Audiences in spontaneous situations engage in wayfinding as well. If you make it easier for your audience to find their way throughout your content, they'll be better able to contextualize and process it.

Research in cognitive neuroscience supports the importance of orienting audiences when communicating. Scholars like to talk about "processing fluency"—how easily and smoothly information gets encoded in our brains. It takes a certain amount of effort for our brains to process random collections of information. Leveraging a structure boosts processing fluency because we don't have to work as hard to make sense of individual pieces of information. As neurologist Josef Parvizi further notes, storytelling works in large part via the creation of mental images in our minds, which our brain processes more quickly than it does abstract ideas. "It's like driving a Porsche rather than taking a bike," he says. Which would you rather use when you're trying to get a message across?[16]

● ● ● TRY IT ● ● ●

Tell a friend about two events you attended recently. Start by listing features of each event. Now turbocharge your message by leveraging the *Comparison–Contrast–Conclusion* road map (reflect on how the events are similar, then on how they're different, then come to some conclusion based on the analysis). In what ways was your response clearer than it might have been had you not used the structure?

Make It Easier for You, Too

If structure influences how our audiences think about the messages we convey, it also impacts our own thinking—structure's fourth benefit. The structure we choose as speakers determines how we think about what we intend to say. Let's imagine we're taking a literature class in college, and a professor calls on us, asking what we thought of the assigned reading for that week, Shakespeare's play *The Tempest*. We could choose to answer that question by comparing it to another of Shakespeare's plays we had read the week earlier. And we could use a structure when delivering our response: *Comparison–Contrast–Conclusion.*

If we hadn't used that particular structure, we might not have focused our thinking on the similarities and differences between the two texts. We might have simply given an opinion of *The Tempest*. Or we might have thought to point to similarities between the two plays but not rigorously analyze the differences. Deploying structures is a way to discipline our thinking. By leading us to adhere to a logic, they force us to stay with a line of argument rather than flit all over the place. They help establish both what we think and ultimately talk about as well as what we don't.

You might presume that disciplining ourselves via structure makes our job as speakers more difficult even as it makes listening easier. Quite the contrary. In spontaneous situations, we have two big problems we must solve: what to say and how to say it. Having a structure solves the "how to say it" part, while also influencing "what to say." When we're telling a story with a logic embedded in it, we know at every point where we've been and where we're going. That frees us to spend more mental energy thinking about the actual content we seek to deliver. It also gives us confidence, especially in spontaneous situations. We don't have to clench our fists silently wondering if we'll come up with something to say after we finish our current thought. We have a road map, so we know we're all set.

To dramatize how much easier spontaneous speaking is when the "how to say it" part is taken care of, I ask my students to throw out random topics on which they would like me to speak. I pause for about fifteen seconds and then deliver a five-minute, impromptu discourse on one of these topics. I spend that fifteen seconds choosing a structure and then very cursorily applying it to the topic. Considering the topic and audience, I ponder whether I might use a persuasive structure like *Problem–Solution–Benefit,* a chronological structure like *Past–Present–Future,* or a comparative structure like *Comparison–Contrast–Conclusion.* To my students' amazement, my speeches actually turn out to be extremely clear and engaging, with minimal effort. Although my long experience with communication obviously helps, my students appreciate how structure can empower them to quickly assemble their thoughts on the fly.

As we become more fluid with structure, opportunities arise for creativity and expressiveness. Since we know where we are in our structure at any given point, we can pause in places to elaborate, experiment, or explore without fearing that we'll become lost. As longtime improvisation instructor James Whittington notes, we can also make impromptu decisions to swap in new ideas, anecdotes, jokes, and so forth as they occur to us at various parts of our structured response, again without worrying that we'll somehow scuttle our larger response.

Of course, we can't indulge ourselves too much in these creative excursions. Whittington recalls that one of his own teachers likened improvisation to driving on a highway: "There are many exits to explore but none are the destination. Take a stroll around the small towns on your long drive, but remember to get back on the highway—don't set up house there and start a family."[17] Structure doesn't free us to go off on endless tangents or endlessly long ones. It doesn't allow us to say absolutely everything that pops into our heads. But it does open up an important space in the moment for us to play around a bit, experiment, and gauge our audiences' reactions.

The Swiss Army Knife of Structures

What would you do if you had to jump in unexpectedly and give a presentation for an absent colleague with only a few minutes' notice? Sarah Zeitler, marketing manager at a publicly traded manufacturing conglomerate, found herself in exactly this situation. Her company was holding a big meeting via videoconference in which it was launching its new products, updating the audience on ongoing projects, and announcing several new acquisitions of other companies. It was Sarah's job to organize the event, which would include short presentations from a number of speakers, and make sure it ran smoothly. More than two hundred people were tuning in to watch the event, including sales reps, subsidiaries of the companies, designers, supervisors, and senior leaders.

In advance of the event, the presenters sent Sarah the PowerPoint slides they would cover. One of them let Sarah know she had a personal errand to run so would log on a few minutes late. Sarah accommodated this colleague by slotting her presentation time toward the end of the program.

On the day of the event, this colleague was more than a few minutes late. Sarah nervously watched the clock. As this woman's presentation time neared, Sarah sent her an email and called her mobile to make sure she was coming. No response.

Sarah took a peek at her colleague's slides—her colleague had planned to update the audience on her ongoing projects, including a new product launch, and the slides were mostly stunning visuals depicting the new product and its features accompanied by just a bit of text. Although Sarah didn't have a deep knowledge of this product or know exactly which of its features her colleague had hoped to cover, she made a split-second decision: she would jump in and present this woman's material.

When it came time for her colleague's presentation to begin, Sarah came on and announced that this woman couldn't make it due to a family conflict. Then she launched into an impromptu presentation. "I took a deep breath," Sarah says, "spoke with confidence, and presented an overview of the incredible work included on the slides." But although Sarah was improvising, she didn't simply cover a series of points at random. She deployed a structure that I taught her called *What–So What–Now What.*

I just *love What–So What–Now What.* It's my favorite structure of all time on account of its simplicity and versatility. You start by discussing an idea, topic, product, service, or argument (What). Then you explain why it's important, helpful, or useful—why it matters and is relevant (So What). You end with what your audience should do from here with this knowledge—how they might apply it, what actions they should take, and so on (Now What).

What–So What–Now What works wonders when giving a spontaneous presentation, answering a question in a job interview, giving a piece of feedback—you name it. If you go back and review this chapter, you'll find that I used *What–So What–Now What* as my organizing schema. After a brief opening, I first described how to define structure (What), then talked about its benefits (So What), and I am now in the midst of talking about how to apply it to what we currently care about, spontaneous speaking (Now What). I think of *What–So What–Now What* as the Swiss Army knife of structures. If you only have time to study and remember one structure, make it this one.

Applying this structure, Sarah first provided basic information about the new product depicted in her colleague's slides and its key features. Then she talked about why these features and benefits mattered. She finished by explaining what needed to happen from here to make the new product launch successful going forward. The structure helped her to stay focused and confident. She took deep breaths and landed her phrases to avoid stutters and ums. "I simply kept going, fueled by my recent focus on presenting with confidence and humility. The audience knew that I wasn't an expert on the topic, but they were still given an opportunity to be updated and were grateful for it." Afterward, senior leaders at the company applauded Sarah's performance, telling her that her presentation was not only well done but incredibly helpful. Upon returning, the original presenter also received accolades for the work that Sarah had presented on her behalf.

Some Classic, All-Purpose Structures[18]

What–So What–Now What
Discuss the topic, why it matters, the practical implications.

Prep (Point, Reason, Example, Point)
Make a point, give the rationale behind it, offer some illustrations, wrap up by returning to the point.

Problem–Solution–Benefit
Evoke an issue, offer a solution, and end by discussing the benefit that your solution will confer.

Comparison–Contrast–Conclusion
When making a comparison, begin by reflecting on the similarities, then the differences, wrapping up your speech by coming to a conclusion.

Situation–Task–Action–Result (STAR)
Describe an event that transpired or evoke a situation, discuss the challenge you had and what you did to address it, end with a discussion of the results you obtained.

Practicing Structure

Sarah was able to jump into this spontaneous situation because she was familiar with the communication structure *What–So What–Now What*. She was able to ask herself those questions about the topic at hand—in this case, her colleague's slide show—and then answered each question out loud in the form of information that she had absorbed through osmosis and through looking at the slides that she had. Whether we know that we need to discuss a specific topic or simply want to be prepared

THINK FASTER, TALK SMARTER

the next time we find ourselves in a group, familiarizing ourselves with a few relevant structures can help us become more comfortable applying them.

We'll cover and apply a number of structures in the second half of this book that can help in specific situations, such as delivering feedback, handling question and answer sessions, making apologies, and offering impromptu toasts. For now, let me say a word about how you might become more comfortable using structures. It's not especially complicated—you adopt a process of practicing that includes repetition, reflection, and feedback. You can't learn a musical instrument by just reading about it. You must play it. Similarly, the first step in learning how to apply structure spontaneously is to *do* it—again and again and again.

When preparing for media events, many leaders will ask themselves similar but varied questions over and over to practice structuring their answers. You might practice generating impromptu speeches using an online tool. Toastmasters, for instance, has a tool that generates questions you can answer. Google has a tool that presents random questions to help you in interview situations.[19] Leverage a generative AI tool like ChatGPT to give you a prompt that you can then use to create a response of your own, using the *What–So What–Now What* formula as your structure.

In addition to practicing the impromptu use of structure, you might also reflect on your efforts, preferably by keeping a journal. After you've practiced, or better yet, after you've tried out structures in real-life conversations, take a moment to think about what worked, what didn't work, and how you might improve going forward.

Many people, I find, tend to focus exclusively on what didn't work, but as I've found in my own practice, it's important to register your successes as well.

Make reflection a regular part of your day—first thing in the morning, perhaps, during your commute home, or before you go to bed at night. Identify one or two communication situations you experienced that day or the previous day, and analyze how you handled them. With whom did you converse most easily? What made it so effortless and fluid? Which structure did you use and why was that so appropriate?

Did you encounter situations in which you wish you had structured your thoughts more clearly? Which structure did you use—and which other structures might have worked better? Were you unsure at times of the other person's message or goal? How might they have used structure more effectively?

At the end of the week, review your journal entries to look for patterns. You might notice, for instance, that you're better spontaneously structuring your communication at certain times of day, when you're with certain colleagues, or in certain settings. Think about why that might be, and what adjustments you might make to create more of the optimal circumstances for your next important conversation.

●●● TRY IT ●●●

The next time you read the news, a book, or some other printed communication, take a few minutes to compose a mini presentation in your mind using the *What–So What–Now What* formula. What was the piece about? How was the information in it important or relevant to you? How can you use that information going forward? This exercise will help you practice structuring the way you think. If you can do that, you will become much more adept at the next step, structuring what you *say*.

In addition to solitary reflection, it's important to consider the impressions of others. Solicit feedback from trusted people in your life, those who you know will be honest with you. Ask these individuals to comment on both the strengths and weaknesses of your structured responses. Solicit their suggestions. Don't just ask, "How did I do?," since that might not lead to frank feedback. Instead ask, "What can I do to be better?"

I've emphasized *What–So What–Now What*, but you can practice structuring your communications using any of the formulas presented in this book as well as others you might find elsewhere. Don't feel compelled to study and practice every last structure you come upon—it's not necessary. Focus on mastering two or three structures that work for you depending on the situations in which you most often find your-

THINK FASTER, TALK SMARTER

self speaking impromptu. You might keep one or two generic structures like *What–So What–Now What* or *Problem–Solution–Benefit* in your back pocket for use in a range of situations, adding a couple of more context-specific structures that you think you'll use frequently.

Prepare for Spontaneity

If you've tuned in to political debates over the past decade, then you've probably had a brush with Karen Dunn. A well-known attorney and longtime specialist in political communication, she helped prepare candidates for several presidential debates. While researching this book, I had a chance to sit down with Dunn and ask her what it takes to perform well spontaneously during a high-pressure situation like a debate. Her answer was unequivocal: preparation.

As she noted, debates, while spontaneous and unscripted, are still highly predictable, which means that practicing for them beforehand can accomplish a lot. "So often," she says, "you can predict what topics are going to be covered and what attacks your opponent will launch. So if you can predict the questions the moderator is going to raise, you can predict what your opponent is going to do, and you're able to practice the most effective interactions."[20] The point isn't to script or memorize what you say. It's to plan for certain contingencies that might materialize, practicing just a few points you might make, stories you might recount, or zingers you might deliver if they do.

Some of the most memorable one-liners in presidential debates—such as "Senator, you're no Jack Kennedy," Lloyd Bentsen's famous response to Dan Quayle in the 1988 vice presidential debate—were roughly envisioned in advance. Debate participants don't know exactly how these moments will come about, but they can predict what types of scenarios they might find themselves in where a good comeback or well-placed joke might come in handy. Given the degree of predictability, top presidential and vice presidential contenders typically put long hours into practicing for debate appearances. They practice on realistic sets with knowledgeable people role-playing their adversaries with considerable accuracy. They usually don't write out verbatim answers to every possible question that others might pose to them, but they do think about topics that will likely come up and nail down several key ideas or messages for each that they wish to convey.

Dunn is hardly the only communications expert who emphasizes the importance of preparation when it comes to spontaneous speaking. Raymond Nasr notes that he counsels his clients to "stockpile stories" in advance, thinking about memorable anecdotes that they can use in certain circumstances. The point, he observes, isn't to memorize these stories word for word but just to have a "catalog of certain stories" that they can call upon in high-pressure situations.[21] Some of the most prominent tech executives Nasr has worked with had a set of stories at their disposal to use as necessary as the occasion demanded. One high-profile leader Nasr worked with wasn't a natural speaker but improved with training. Developing a reservoir of stories from his own life and about famous historical figures "gave him comfort because he could just push rewind and play and he knew it would go over well."

As we've seen earlier in the book, we go astray with spontaneous speaking when we plan too closely and aim for some notion of perfection. But the fact that we're operating without a script doesn't mean we can't prepare. On the contrary, the best impromptu speakers I've seen *do* prepare, and they do so with great commitment and intensity. They practice techniques for overcoming anxiety and develop a toolbox of tactics for calming down in the moment. They practice skills such as listening and introspection. And as I've suggested in this chapter, they develop a small but potent catalog of structures that they can call upon in specific situations to respond in ways that are clear, directed, engaging, and "sticky."

Spontaneous communication in daily life might be unscripted, but like political debates, they aren't random. We can often anticipate how we'll feel, what various contexts and speaking situations will demand of us, what kind of content our audiences might want to hear, and how we might most compellingly present it to them. By familiarizing ourselves with structures and practicing their application, we put ourselves in a position to shine when it really counts, just as we do by taking the other preemptive steps described in this book. We might even find ourselves doing something wonderful we never quite expected: having fun while speaking in the moment.

● ● ● **DRILL IT** ● ● ●

1. Imagine you're giving a tourist advice on where to go when visiting your city. List three or four attractions they might see or experience. Now give the same advice or guidance, but convey it as a story of some kind based on your experiences. Think about which of the two approaches is more compelling, memorable, or useful for your audience and why.

2. The "Story Spine" is a class exercise from the world of improvisation, and you can use it to practice structuring information as a story.[22] Fill in the following prompt to set up a scenario, including characters and time and place:
    *   "Once upon a time . . . [insert character and place]"
    *   "Every day . . . [describe normal life]."
    *   "But, one day . . . [insert event] happened."
    *   "Because of that . . . [insert another event] happened."
    *   "Because of [insert yet another event] happened."
    *   [Add more events . . .]
    *   "Until, finally . . . [insert final action]."
    *   "And, ever since then . . . [insert change that has taken place]."

    Using this format, create two or three narratives. Are you starting to get more of a feel for storytelling? The more you do this, the easier it will be to create narratives on the spot.

3. Use the electronic tools for generating questions mentioned in this chapter to practice applying structure, using one of the five all-purpose structures I outlined earlier.

Chapter 6: Focus

THE F-WORD
OF SPONTANEOUS SPEAKING

Don't make it hard for your audiences to "get" your point.
Focus their attention on what matters most.

The best, most powerful communication in both formal and spontaneous situations is clear and sharply *focused*. It conveys everything an audience needs to receive the speaker's desired message—and only that information. It doesn't distract audience members, bore them, or waste their time by using verbiage that is fuzzy, irrelevant, impossibly dense, acronym-laden, or long-winded.

For a classic example of a well-focused albeit painstakingly planned message, consider how Steve Jobs first introduced Apple's revolutionary iPod to the world. The year was 2001, the occasion a press briefing held at an auditorium at the company's headquarters. Upon taking the stage, Jobs could have raved about the iPod's many features—its sleek design, its weight, the size of its screen, how much storage capacity it offered. Instead he beguiled consumers with a focused, memorable message that in just five words conveyed everything they wanted and needed to know about Apple's new product: "1,000 songs in your pocket."[1]

At the time, many music lovers stored their music on CDs, which were cumbersome to lug around. Other MP3 players existed, but they had a limited storage capacity. The phrase "1,000 songs in your pocket," which became a tagline for Apple's advertising, accomplished several tasks at once. It evoked consumers' previous challenges in listening to music, distinguished the iPod from the competition, and conveyed the iPod's practical value for consumers—all in five simple words. The iPod went on to become hugely popular. It revolutionized the way we listen to music and also gave rise to the whole medium of podcasting (something for which I am very grateful).

I wish more communication in everyday life were as sharply focused and meaningful as this bit of marketing magic was. How often have you chatted with someone at a cocktail party only to find yourself in the middle of an anecdote with so much backstory that you forgot why they even started telling it? How often have leaders at your company answered questions in ways that seemed confusing and vague? How often have colleagues, customer service agents, friends, or others in your life danced around an issue, making elaborate excuses to avoid responsibility, providing excessive background information to establish their authority, or chattering on simply to hear themselves speak?

We don't always realize it when our messages lack focus—but others do.

One leader my firm was brought in to coach, the founder of a gaming company, was fielding questions during a public presentation focused on building enthusiasm for the company's new product launch. An audience member asked a technical question about a feature that was missing from the company's products. The founder went on for twenty minutes, walking the audience through the company's thinking about this technical detail and the various ways its engineers might handle it.

His answer was truthful and comprehensive, and it even followed a clear structure. Unfortunately, it conveyed information relevant to only a tiny number of people in the audience, and not the key demographic that he was trying to reach. As a result, most audience members tuned out after a few minutes. What the leader had missed in that moment was to focus on the information that the primary audience needed, and answer the question in a way that would be relevant to the majority; had he done that, he might have realized he needed to answer the question more simply, saying something like "Yes, that feature will be in our product's next release."

We need not be communication geniuses like Steve Jobs to maintain a sharp focus, nor must we masterfully sculpt every last word in advance so that it's "just right." As with structure, just a bit of practice and skills development goes a long way, empowering us to deliver more focused messages impromptu. My work with clients and students has led me to identify *four dimensions or qualities of focused messages*: precision, relevance, accessibility, and concision. Practice enhancing these qualities and you'll find yourself connecting better with audiences, engaging them longer, and delivering messages that stick better in people's minds.

Dimension #1—Precision: "Um, What's the Point Exactly?"
Bottom Line: Have a clear goal—know, feel, do.

Focused messages are nothing if not precise, tailored to have a specific effect or impact. When we're precise, we know exactly what we hope to accomplish in the course of speaking and we craft our language to achieve that end. This begs the question: What *do* we hope to accomplish? Many times, we have only a vague or partial sense. As a result, we struggle to determine not only what to say, but what *not* to say. This leads us to respond in ways that distract audiences, confuse them, or bore them to oblivion.

When most people reflect on their communication goals, they consider information they wish to impart or ideas they hope to convey—in other words, their content. But what we want our audience to *know* is only one dimension of our goals as communicators. We must also consider what we want audiences to *feel*, the emotions we want them to experience. And we must consider what we want our audiences to *do*, the actions we want our audiences to take. A goal isn't simply our intended meaning but also the broader impact we intend that meaning to have.

Clarity across all three dimensions of our communication goal can be extremely powerful. Audiences can more easily grasp our intended meaning, and we as speakers can adapt to almost any situation that might arise, even those that would ordinarily become total train wrecks.

When people craft goals, they tend to ignore emotions, and they also tend to remain vague about the actions they want to see. So let's first consider emotions. As we saw in chapter 5, stories lodge in our memories more easily and get into our brains faster than other information because they trigger emotions, becoming meaningful in ways that statistics and bullet points can't. Marketers know the power of emotion well. If they connect with consumers on the level of feelings, consumers tend to buy more and stay more attached to the brand. Leveraging Nobel laureate Daniel Kahneman's work in behavioral economics, marketing professor Baba Shiv speculates that "something like ninety to ninety-five percent of our decisions [. . . and] our behaviors are constantly being shaped nonconsciously by [our] emotional brain system."[2] One study found that customers who were "fully connected" to companies on an emotional level were over 50 percent more valuable to them in economic terms than those who just felt "highly satisfied" with their products.[3]

You'll notice that in this last paragraph, I didn't follow my own advice: I tried to convince you to pay closer attention to emotion when thinking about your goals as a communicator, but I did it by appealing to your rational mind, citing data points and scientific studies. Let me rectify that. Picture yourself sitting in a conference room at work. It's almost five o'clock on a Friday and you're eager for your weekend to start. You're in your last meeting of the day—a presentation by one of your bosses. The point of the presentation is simple—there's a big market opportunity that your team can seize—but your boss has bogged down his presentation with charts and tables. Imagine how impatient you're getting as he painstakingly explains yet another slide, and another. When someone asks a question, your boss responds impromptu with—yes—still more data points and rational arguments piled atop one another. A ball of tension forms in your stomach as you struggle to stay awake and not fidget. You find yourself asking: Why do I care about this? What am I supposed to do with this information? Your boss hasn't clarified the dimension of his goals, and it is unclear what he wants anybody to do next.

Did this more emotional, story-driven articulation of my argument feel more compelling to you than my earlier sentences laden with data and quotations from authority?

Beyond information and emotion, we must consider action. We tend to remain fuzzy on the specific actions we wish our audiences to take as a result of our messages. I see this all the time when prep-ping entrepreneurs for informal question and answer sessions. Many of them know what information they wish to convey (for instance, data about the company's mission, strong past performance, and future op-portunities) as well as the emotional impact (in most cases, curiosity and excitement about the firm). But they don't always make it clear what they want their audiences to do. Entrepreneurs will tell me they seek to obtain "support" for their ventures. What does that mean ex-actly? Is it financial investment? Is it getting someone to like them on social media? Is it getting audience members to become evangelists for the company? If they haven't thought this through carefully enough, they can't fine-tune what they're saying in a way that leads audience members in the desired direction. They find it harder to respond in the moment, and their impromptu messages don't hang together.

To improve your ability to speak spontaneously, you would do well to first clarify your goals in your own mind. If you're about to enter a situation where you think you might speak spontaneously, spend a few minutes jotting down answers to three questions:

- What do you want people to know?
- What do you want them to feel?
- What do you want them to do?

● ● ● TRY IT ● ● ●

Think back to the last time you spoke spontaneously. What did you want people to know, feel, and do? Were the messages you delivered aligned with these goals?

Think about how you might measure success. Will your audience be able to understand a given set of ideas? Will you see visible signs that they feel a certain way? Will the audience give you a certain amount of money or take another action a given number of times?

After speaking spontaneously, take a few minutes to evaluate how successful you were, comparing the impact you had to your previously established goals. Did you achieve your goal across all three areas? Why or why not? What might you do better next time? If you run through this exercise a few times, you'll get in the habit of entering social situations with more precise ambitions and analyzing your behavior afterward more rigorously.

Dimension #2—Relevance: "Why Should I Care?"
Bottom Line: Focus on importance and salience for your audience.

Legendary entrepreneur Jim Koch, a pioneer of craft brewing and the creator of Samuel Adams Boston Lager, knows a thing or two about selling. Early in his career, he and his business partner got their company, the Boston Beer Company, off the ground by going into neighborhood bars one at a time and making their pitch. Sometimes they succeeded, often they did not. Looking back on his career, Koch relates his belief in what he calls the "Golden Rule of Selling": "Never ask customers to do something that is not in their long-term best interest."[4]

Underlying that rule, Koch suggests, is an extreme focus on the customer. "Businesses should adhere to an almost Buddhist ideal of selflessness," he says. "If you do that, as we did from the outset, you make life a lot easier for yourself. You build trusting, loyal relationships with people. You wind up winning financially because your customers benefit from the relationship. And perhaps most importantly, you feel good about selling because you are helping others succeed as well."

To sell in a selfless way, you must first strive to understand customers and their concerns. "Take time to listen carefully and understand what customers perceive their need to be," Koch counsels. "Until you understand people's reasons for doing what they're doing, you have no ability to change their beliefs and behavior. You're just arguing, and you're not going to win."

Koch relates the challenge he faced every time he walked into a bar on a sales call. Within thirty seconds, he had to size up the person with whom he was meeting as well as the bar and its business. Only then could he figure out how to pitch his product to them. And if he couldn't think of a way that Samuel Adams Boston Lager could fill the bar's needs and contribute to its success, he didn't try too hard to push it. He continued on to the next bar.

● ● ● TRY IT ● ● ●

A famous improvisation game called "sell a blank to a blank" asks participants to sell a random product and service to a randomly selected type of person. The product might be a plunger or a piano, and the job type or person might be a police officer, circus clown, or kindergarten teacher. The person playing this game would spend a minute or two trying to sell a plunger to a police officer, for instance, or a piano to a circus clown. This game helps us to practice imagining other people and tailoring our communication to their needs. Try picking three products or services of your own. For each one, pick a type of person to sell to. How might you best frame your pitch?

Creating Common Ground

The strongest, most focused messages are those that audiences perceive as relevant to their situations. They are messages that speak directly to who audiences are, what they want, and what they need—messages that somehow address the question that lingers in the mind of any of us when we're listening: "Why should I care?"

We often go astray in spontaneous situations by failing to craft our message with audiences in mind. We assume that the people we are speaking to have a base-level interest for what we want to talk about, simply because of our own enthusiasm for the topic. We focus on what *we* want to say, without asking ourselves how to frame the message in a context that our audience wants or needs to hear. When we're trying to argue for an idea, we rattle off arguments that are important and impactful to us. Particularly when discussing a topic that we feel emotionally about, we may skip the step of asking what will make the same topic important, impactful, and emotionally resonant for our audience. Ditto when we're trying to sell a product or service: we list the features and functions rather than explaining how what we're selling solves an important problem or challenge as customers define it.

To make your spontaneous communication more relevant, make a habit of thinking about your audiences and their needs. You can do this in the moment. If someone puts you on the spot with a question, pause for just a second and ask yourself, "Who is this person? What do they need to hear? How can I frame what I'm about to say so that it's most relevant/interesting/urgent for them?"

If you're heading into a situation where you might have to speak spontaneously, spend a little time beforehand preparing with some base-level questions. You can even perform a slightly more rigorous analysis, grounded, if possible, in some quick research. Consider the following questions:

- How might I best convey to this particular audience what I find most important or compelling about my topic?
- How much does the audience know about my topic?
- What impressions of me and my topic does my audience likely have?
- Are there any likely areas of resistance, concern, or hesitation?
- What motivates my audience?

Let's say you're in a wedding party for a close friend who grew up on the other side of the country. You don't know your friend's family very well, and you've never met their fiancé's family. You do know that your friend comes from a community that holds traditional religious beliefs and that shows great deference to its elders. Because you're such close friends, you think it likely that someone will invite you to toast the happy couple at some point during the multiday event.

You might ponder the previous questions as you prepare to speak. The likelihood is that the audience doesn't know you, so you'll need to spend at least a little time describing who you are and what your friend means to you. You'll also need to spend a little time thinking about your audience. Perhaps you have learned that it is customary in your friend's culture to show deference to their elders, so you could consider expressing how meaningful it has been to meet your friend's parents. When you're giving a toast to a room with a range of ages and acquaintances, you should consider what kind of humor will get laughs versus what might create discomfort in the room. Think critically about how your audience might respond to anything inappropriate. Ultimately, you know that your audience is motivated by love for your friend, so you should think of a couple of endearing stories to tell that captures your own affection for them.

Putting in just a few minutes of thought along these lines can pay huge dividends when you're put on the spot. You might not respond perfectly, but the messages you craft will be more meaningful and relevant and less likely to cause offense than if you hadn't considered your audience prior. Further, if you pose these questions and realize that you don't know the answers, you can take steps to gain more insight into your audience, for instance by speaking quickly with your friend and asking them about their family.

Another way to find common ground with an audience and establish the relevance of your ideas is to deliberately create moments of curiosity or tension. Let's say you're on a Zoom call when your manager asks for your thoughts on how your team might update one of the company's current products. In a situation like this, you may feel put on the spot—especially if you know that some customers have provided negative feedback. But rather than hide from that reality, a situation like this could give you an opportunity. In answering your boss's query, you might spur curiosity in your boss and others on the Zoom by first identifying three or four unexpected comments you've received from customers about their experiences with your product. Hearing this feedback might trigger questions in the minds of your audience members. How did these comments originate? How might we best address them? Is there an opportunity to improve or expand? If the customer feedback you're citing was negative, bringing it up might create tension among the group, but you can transform that tension into curiosity by establishing a new, shared priority—how might we resolve this problem? Posing this question might create a sense of urgency, priming audience members to find your response to your boss's original query—"How might the team update the company's current product?"—more relevant and interesting.

● ● ● **TRY IT** ● ● ●

In your next spontaneous encounter, try creating a moment of curiosity for your audience that might make the topic seem more relevant and urgent. If someone poses a question for you to answer on the spot, create just a bit of uncertainty by first defining a potential impact or challenge that the answer you'll give will address, and only then delivering the answer itself. If someone hasn't asked a question but you find yourself in the position of communicating an idea, evoke curiosity by first posing and answering a question of your own. For example, when you spontaneously need to share information about a new product, you could ask, "Do we really want to support two products in the market?"

Turning Resistance into Curiosity

The example above demonstrates how thinking about relevance requires that we also address potential areas of resistance that audience members might have. We can also do this by dampening the tension, moderating our words so as not to say something that we know will set off the audience. "Any time you're thinking about resistance and how to combat it, you're really thinking about defensiveness," Social psychologist and Stanford GSB professor Zakary Tormala observes. Our challenge is to help reduce that defensiveness in others. "So taking a more open, agreeable, inclusive, and cooperative type approach with people generally lowers their resistance, and then you have a chance. At least there's some wiggle room." To project more openness and inclusivity, we can ask questions and try to find common ground. We might say something like, "In thinking about how to achieve this goal, I am curious about your thoughts on X."

Every bit of effort we take to increase relevance increases the odds that our audiences will engage with our message. The reality is that most audiences are selfish with their attention and focus. This holds even in spontaneous situations where people appear to be motivated to hear what you have to say. Interviewers are curious about your answers;

colleagues seeking feedback want to hear your thoughts; audience members at celebrations want to hear your toast. Yet these folks still can become distracted and fail to pay attention. They'll stand a better chance of tuning in if your communication seems important to *them* and well tailored to their needs. Address the "Why should *I* care" question in the course of communicating and you'll find that audiences really will care more about what you say—and they'll pay attention to your focused message.

Dimension #3—Accessibility: "Why Is This Stuff So Complicated?"
Bottom Line: Make your content understandable by avoiding jargon and acronyms.

One of the most common mistakes we make in spontaneous communication is to overcommunicate. In line with the importance of listening to the room and thinking ahead about what kind of communication our audience is ready to have, many of us could stand to make our spontaneous communication more accessible. Complexity can stand in the way of some of our most important conversations.

Some of this complexity occurs because people feel the need to broadcast their status as experts. A great deal of it owes to what some have called the "curse of knowledge": we know too much for our own good, and we make assumptions and use language when communicating that our audiences or frankly most ordinary mortals would find impenetrable.[5] There is also what we might call the "curse of passion": we ramble on unnecessarily, conveying everything we know about a subject, simply because we feel passionately about the topic at hand and presume our audience does, too.

But complexity comes at a cost, especially in spontaneous situations. Complexity renders our messages confusing and distracting. In many cases, it can turn our audiences off by creating needless distance between ourselves and them—we're the experts, and they're just lowly, uninformed listeners. Finally, it can make our communication much longer than it should be, leading audience members to become overwhelmed or bored and tune out.

When you become aware of complexity's sheer prevalence in society and our obliviousness to it, it can seem almost farcical. I got a laugh some years ago when leading a workshop for members of the U.S. military. I was explaining how detrimental complex language, jargon, and acronyms were for communicators when a military official raised his hand and said that he and his colleagues didn't have a problem with excessive jargon. I was flabbergasted, observing that in the short time I'd been with them I'd heard a whole array of acronyms whose meaning escaped me. "Well," this gentleman said, "we have a goat for that."

I had no clue what he was talking about. "A goat? You sacrifice an animal and everyone somehow understands acronyms? You write acronyms on an animal and that's how everyone learns?"

He explained that he was talking about a GOAT, not a goat. GOAT stood for "Glossary of Acronyms and Terms." Apparently, all newcomers to the team I was addressing received a copy of the GOAT so that they could understand what their colleagues were talking about. Here, in other words, was a professional environment in which acronyms, jargon, and complex langauge were so prevalent that they had created a handbook to compile and explain it all—and even that handbook's name was an acronym! It didn't occur to them to try a different and far more elegant solution: pare back the complicated language so that both spontaneous and formal communication were more accessible.

TED Talks are a standard eighteen minutes long. As curator Chris Anderson has remarked, this length is "short enough to hold people's attention, including on the Internet, and precise enough to be taken seriously. But it's also long enough to say something that matters."[6] As it turns out, speakers really don't need a full eighteen minutes. The late Hans Rosling, coauthor of the book *Factfulness* and a well-regarded TED speaker, demonstrated in 2012 that it's possible to hold someone's attention and "say something that matters" in under a minute. And guess what? He did it while mostly speaking spontaneously.

In a moment captured on video and billed as "the shortest TED [T]alk ever given," Rosling identified what he felt would become a burning global issue in the years to come: the challenge posed by economic inequality coupled with population growth. He held up seven stones, indicating that each represents one billion of the earth's population, which at the time was seven billion. He placed one stone on the ground—this represented the billion people affluent enough to travel abroad. He placed another stone on the ground—this represented another billion people affluent enough to secure access to a car. He placed three more stones on the ground, representing the three billion who could afford to save up for a bike or motorcycle. Then two more stones went onto the ground—this was the next tranche of the earth's population that could afford to save only for a pair of shoes.

With this setup in place, Rosling noted that in the years to come, the global population would become more affluent. Rearranging stones, he observed that people at the lower rungs of global society would move up—one billion would still be able to afford airfare, while three billion would afford access to a car and another three billion would be able to aspire to own a bike. Few would be poor enough to aspire to buy only a pair of shoes. Then he added three more stones to the mix, noting that the global population would one day soon rise to ten billion, with all of the population heading up to the top two economic rungs.

"The question," he observed, in his presentation's rousing conclusion, "is whether the rich people over there are prepared to be integrated [with the formerly poor] in a world with ten billion people." There it was, an important insight conveyed in mere seconds. "That is the shortest TED Talk ever given," Rosling proclaimed with a smile.

Rosling could have cited all kinds of facts and figures. He could have trotted out the names of famous economists and others studying the issue. He could have pointed to classic theorists of population growth. He could have made reference to obscure terms of art, such as "crude birth rate" or "doubling time" or the "push-pull hypothesis."[7] But for his audience, a general one comprised of nonspecialists, all of that would have been distracting and beside the point. Rosling retained remarkable focus in the moment by keeping his remarks not only relevant but as clear and accessible as possible.

We don't all have to be geniuses of clear and accessible communication—it's enough to simply take steps to improve our game. Justin Kestler, a founder of the popular literature study guide series LitCharts who was the original editor in chief of SparkNotes and now also leads CliffsNotes, thinks of such products as serving not so much to pare down long, complex works of literature but rather to analyze and explain their themes so that the works can be understood and appreciated more easily by the broader public. We likewise can think of ourselves as translators whose job it is to put complex ideas into relatively straightforward terms that anyone can understand.[8] Just a bit of attention to translation can go a long way, helping us deliver more focused messages on the spot.

To reduce jargon, we might make a habit of putting ourselves in someone else's shoes. Just before we say something, or if we're about to enter a situation where we anticipate having to speak spontaneously, we can think about our audience and their capacity to understand. When I explain technology to members of my family, I apply what we in my family call the "grandmother test." My elderly mother doesn't have much knowledge of the latest gadgets. How can I explain technology— minimizing jargon and keeping technical explanations and detail to a minimum—so she can gain a practical understanding of it? Even when I'm not speaking with my mom, I can apply the grandmother test to ensure that I'm not overwhelming my audience with unnecessary complexity, either.

If you aren't sure about your audience's capacity to understand, do some quick research. The toymaker LEGO is widely known for creating instruction manuals so simple and accessible that kids anywhere— including those who haven't learned to read yet—can use them to build their desired projects. LEGO designer Anthony Dalby told me that the company maintains a "very, very deep knowledge and understanding of what kids are able to understand at any age."[9] It uses that knowledge to make decisions such as how many LEGO bricks it shows on a page of an instruction manual or how to color the bricks. It painstakingly imparts this knowledge to employees, requiring that they undergo a full year of training before they can write building instructions.

As spontaneous communicators, we cannot usually count on having this depth of understanding of our audience. But it does help to know in advance if our audiences are familiar with certain words or concepts, how long they are liable to pay attention, how they like to receive information, and so on. If you're appearing at a professional or company function, a quick chat with the organizer or an employee at the company might be all that you need to get this information. If applicable, you might also hop online and see the kind of language the company uses on its own website or that company leaders or representatives used at previous appearances that were recorded and posted.

I recommend running a quick diagnostic of your communication on a periodic basis to ensure that you're not drowning others in acronyms and excessive details. If you've just attended a conference, cocktail party, or some other event in which you've spoken spontaneously, take a few moments to replay these conversations in your mind. Did you use any jargon? Did you take time to explain and deconstruct your ideas in the course of delivering your message?

● ● ● **TRY IT** ● ● ●

Think about the shorthand, jargon, or industry vocabulary you most often use. Over a period of a few days, notice when you use these terms, and think of more accessible synonyms you might use in conversation with others. Set yourself a *jargon challenge* and see whether you can go an entire day without using these terms.

You might object that the nature of your work or hobbies requires you to convey complex concepts or esoteric ideas to others. What can you do then? Just as you might take time in advance to prepare a set of stories to have in your back pocket in spontaneous situations, you might also think in advance of some key strategies to deploy in the moment to cut to the essence of an idea and render it accessible. These strategies might include clever or colorful analogies you can use by way of explanation, or if you anticipate standing in front of a whiteboard, an easy visual you might draw to convey the essence of the idea.[10] You could also chunk down your idea into a few basic, easy-to-understand concepts or steps—a strategy Kestler used in creating LitCharts.

By the way, this chunking approach is a neat way of helping audiences connect better with what you're saying. People who aren't especially motivated to receive a message tend to remember most of the information they hear at the start of your communication, tuning out the rest. By chunking a message, you're in effect creating multiple starting moments, enabling your audience to stay more engaged throughout and to remember more of the overall message.[11]

One especially important strategy to consider in advance is conveying the most important information up front. Journalists capture this method with the phrase "Don't bury the lead." In other words, start an article with the big news item stated in simple form *and then* go on to give increasing amounts of detail. In the military, this technique is known as BLUF (yes, an acronym . . . I know): Bottom Line Up Front. Organizing information in this way can focus audiences quickly on the main message, saving them from having to dig through a morass of detail. (Did you notice I used BLUF for each of the four dimensions in this chapter?) Practicing the delivery of your ideas in BLUF prior to a meeting or conference can help you become much more focused when you find yourself on the spot. It can also help to ask yourself the question "What do I *really* want to say?" when you're speaking in the moment, as this helps you to prioritize your thoughts.

Dimension #4—Concision: "Why Are They So Long-Winded?" *Bottom Line: Be crisp.*

From her reading of parenting books, my wife learned a mantra that she reminds me of as we're working out issues with our kids: "Minimal words." When I ask one of our kids to do something they don't want to do, I tend to explain a rationale to them . . . and explain it . . . and explain it. My wife simply tells our kids what to do—"Join us at seven p.m. for dinner," "Clean up your room"—with little or no explanation. By saying less, she finds that she creates fewer opportunities for challenges and endless discussion. Conflict situations get resolved more quickly and efficiently. Life in our household becomes more harmonious.

My wife might be on to something. As neurologist Josef Parvizi told me, concision makes messages easier to receive, as it activates fewer processing systems in the brain.[12] Uttering fewer words will usually allow us to connect better with audiences and keep their attention. In our age of rapidly shrinking attention spans, audiences have little patience for bloated messages. We must ask ourselves: Is everything we're saying—every idea, sentence, or word—really necessary? Or might we be able to convey even relatively simple, accessible concepts more quickly and efficiently without sacrificing clarity and relevance?

In fact, leveraging the context in which we're communicating often can help us reduce our word count even further. When we're strolling with a friend into a library or museum, we don't need to tell our friend to "speak quietly"—it's obvious. Likewise, when we're headed to a funeral, we don't need to tell others in our group to show respect and tone down what they're saying. The atmosphere itself will usually convey the social expectations.

The cartoonist Hilary Price, creator of the award-winning, daily, single-panel comic strip *Rhymes with Orange*, relies on the context of the images she creates to tell entire stories using only a handful of words. Every object in her panels—a cloud, a bush, a piece of furniture—is carefully designed to help her convey her message. Every word counts, too. "The thing you want to do," she says, "is use the fewest number of words you can and let a picture tell the story. You never want to say 'apple' if you could show an apple."

As part of her creative process, Price starts with more words in a panel and winnows them down as she refines her work. She also tries to convey as little information as possible, allowing readers room to draw connections themselves. As she observes, a great deal of pleasure in reading a comic strip comes in piecing together the meaning, or as she puts it, "going from not knowing to knowing." Of course, she can't give too little information—that would only confuse readers. The trick is to reach a sweet spot of concision *and* clarity. In her mind, she can accomplish that by conveying only 49 percent of the information, leaving it to readers to fill in the rest based on the context in which they encounter her messages.

Often, she'll achieve that concision by depicting a scene just before an event happens, leaving it to readers to draw logical conclusions about what will soon transpire.

"What's funnier," she says, "watching me throw a drink at you or seeing me as I'm just about to do that?" The latter, of course—and there's no need to then show the actual throwing of the drink or the reactions of the characters afterward. The ancient Greeks held that "brevity is the soul of wit" (an antecedent to our own aphorism "less is more"). In Price's world, brevity is the soul of humor and entertainment. The take away: Leverage context and consider the least amount of information you would need to convey your meaning clearly. Then stick to that.

We can also attack verbosity directly by becoming more aware of how we respond when put on the spot. *New York Times* editor Glenn Kramon advises writers to read their work aloud to find opportunities for more concision. As speakers, we can do the opposite. If we're speaking in a room or on a Zoom and someone is recording it, we can go back after the fact and analyze a written transcript of what we said (or consult the recording itself), noticing patterns in our speech—repetition of sentences, presentation of excessive detail, and so on—that add unnecessary verbiage. We can also have a partner ask us questions, record our spontaneous responses, and analyze them afterword for patterns. Before we enter situations in which we anticipate speaking impromptu, we can remind ourselves not to repeat these patterns. And we can continue to watch recordings of ourselves periodically to check in on our progress.

An even simpler way to self-assess is to review your text messages from the past week. Most of these likely constitute spontaneous communication on your part, albeit in written rather than spoken form. Were your responses longer or more numerous than necessary? Were you saying more than those with whom you were corresponding? What patterns of verbosity did you notice? Challenge yourself over the next week to write fewer and shorter but more meaningful texts and notice how it impacts your relationships with others.

It might also help to tackle what we can call "brevity challenges." The next time you're preparing to enter a spontaneous speaking situation, think about your primary messages and see how it feels to convey them as a tweet, sticking to the original 140-character limit. Doing this regularly can enhance your ability to focus your message and keep it short. You might also practice writing haikus, poems composed of only seventeen syllables. Or you might try your hand at writing a short-short story (believe it or not, some people can write a complete story in only six words) or delivering a PechaKucha presentation (a format in which you're limited to twenty slides and twenty seconds of discussion per slide).[13]

● ● ● **TRY IT** ● ● ●

Take your first brevity challenge: summarize this chapter in twenty-five words or less. Can you do it? Now try brevity challenges in other aspects of your life.

A $1.5 Trillion Company in Just Twelve Words

As of late 2023, Google (now called Alphabet) is one of the world's most valuable companies, with a market value exceeding $1.2 trillion.[14] It has numerous businesses, including in online search, cloud computing, consumer electronics, AI, and even quantum computing. It operates out of dozens of locations around the world. Yet despite the company's size and complexity, Google's leadership has been able to boil what the company does down to just twelve words. As Google's mission statement informs us, the company aims "to organize the world's information and make it universally accessible and useful."

This mission is a simple statement that most people can readily understand. But arriving at such a sharply focused phrasing was not so simple. Raymond Nasr helped to craft this mission statement during the early 2000s while serving as the company's director of communication. As he recalls, he and other colleagues met monthly for three hours at a time to crack exactly how to convey Google's business purpose. It was a tough challenge. They needed a phrase that not only conveyed what the company was about but was also concise, repeatable, and optimistic and came from a place of passion.

"We worked so long and hard on it—it became a labor of love," Nasr says. "We revised and revised and revised until we were blue in the face. It was no fun at all, but when you love a company, you do it."[15] Finally, after many months, they were able to arrive at a wording that pleased the firm's founders, Larry Page and Sergey Brin. The company formally adopted "to organize the world's information and make it universally accessible and useful" as its mission. As of this writing in 2023, Google still presents this same formulation publicly on its website.[16]

In our spontaneous communication, achieving focus can be harder than it looks. You might come away from this chapter wondering how you'll ever do it. It's tough enough improving in the other areas covered in this book: managing anxiety, relinquishing perfectionism, reframing how we approach spontaneous communication, listening better to others, and lending structure to what we say. Now that we're working on all of that, how can we also work on four additional areas related to focus? Won't we overwhelm ourselves and risk *losing* focus in the very act of trying to find it as communicators?

It's a valid question, and I have what I hope is an equally valid answer: take it slow. Although improving along all four dimensions will help you take your focus to the max, you need not do it all at once. Work on one dimension of focus at a time. Just a bit of attention here can enhance your self-awareness in the moment, leading to much clearer, more powerful messages.

Remember, there is no "perfect" when it comes to communication generally, and focus in particular. We can take each of the four dimensions of focus too far. If we're too goal-directed, we can become rigid, unable to respond to the shifting demands of a spontaneous situation. Think of the politician in a debate who just harps repetitively on their points without acknowledging questions others are asking. If we spend too much time tailoring our message for our audience, it risks becoming overly narrow, tailored *only* to them and utterly uninteresting to anyone else. If we push accessibility too far, it might seem as if we're dumbing down our messages and making them too simple. If we're too concise, we risk confusing our audiences—they don't have enough information or detail to understand what we're trying to say.

Remaining mindful of the F-word of communication and drawing our audience's attention to what matters most will dramatically improve the power of our messages. We want audiences to hear us. We want to create common ground with them. And it's up to us to make their job as easy, pain-free, and interesting as possible. The more we share our ideas, the more we listen and learn about our audiences, the better able we will be to focus our messages so that they powerfully resonate.

● ● ● **DRILL IT** ● ● ●

1. Think about the last meeting you attended. Try to summarize it in fifty words, then twenty-five words, and then twelve. What did you do to cut back the words? Did you focus on reducing jargon? On reducing complexity? How did you prioritize what you communicated?

2. Pick a topic about which you feel passionately, and jot down a few notes reflecting what you would say about this topic if someone gave you two or three minutes to speak. Imagine speaking before a group that is completely engaged with that topic; then imagine speaking before a group to whom you are introducing this topic for the very first time. Consider how you might adjust your remarks to reflect the varying needs of these audiences. What more might you add in each case and what might you subtract to keep each engaged and interested?

3. Think of a fairly complex task you perform in your daily life, such as putting a child to bed, shuffling cards, preparing your favorite dish, or negotiating a business arrangement. Think of how you might describe this task using a metaphor or analogy (for example, "Putting a child to bed is like . . ."). Now practice describing this task in front of a mirror or camera. Does the metaphor or analogy allow you to describe the task more simply and in fewer words?

PART II

Talking Smarter in Specific Situations

As we saw in chapter 5, understanding structure is vital to doing well in spontaneous speaking situations. Structure functions much like prep work does for a chef. If we've taken time beforehand to choose a recipe (in other words, a structure), to think it through, and to perform the attendant chopping and slicing and organizing of ingredients, all we'll need to do in the moment is actually assemble the dish. Of course, the recipe we choose will vary depending on the situation (we wouldn't want to prepare filet mignon, say, for a casual weeknight dinner). In this portion of the book, I examine a range of common speaking challenges and present simple "recipes" or ways of organizing what we say as well as some additional tips for communicating at our best. Practice these structures, and we'll turbocharge our efforts to think faster and talk smarter.

Special note: You might have bypassed part I of this book and skipped right to this section. That's perfectly fine, but I do hope you'll go back at some point to read part I as well. What you'll find here will help you to speak spontaneously in specific communication situations. Part I will teach you a methodology for becoming comfortable with spontaneous communication, regardless of the goal or setting. These general techniques are essential if you really want to master the art of in-the-moment communication.

Application #1

GOING BIG ON SMALL TALK

Key Insight

Networking and small-talk situations—the epitome of spontaneous speaking—make many of us cringe. Initiating and exiting these brief, informal encounters can feel incredibly awkward. During the encounters themselves, most of us feel as if we never quite know what to say and how to say it. We want to seem witty and interesting, but chatting breezily with others—whether at informal cocktail parties, corporate all-hands meetings, mixers at professional conferences, events at our kid's school, or at many other gatherings—can seem like an endless verbal tennis match of spontaneous remarks, queries, and feedback. It need not be this way. With some cognitive reframing, a useful structure, and some specific guiding principles in hand, we can learn not just to survive small talk but to actually enjoy it.

Why It Matters

Small talk might seem trivial, but it can deliver big results. First, it can help us to forge new or deeper connections with others by allowing us to discover unexpected areas of common interest.[1] Second, it can give us a chance to test out potential relationships, helping us determine if we'd like to move them forward. Third, it can enable us to establish or reinforce our personal reputations, giving us an opportunity to demonstrate warmth and empathy—skills that friends and colleagues value highly. Finally, small talk helps us see whether anyone in the room might share our personal or professional goals and aspirations. For all of these reasons, we owe it to ourselves not to shrink from small talk, but to find ways to cultivate the gift of gab. Focusing on structure is an excellent way forward.

Craft Your Content

My favorite formula to use when engaging in informal, spontaneous conversations is one we discussed in chapter 5: *What–So What–Now What*. First you make an argument or point (What), next you describe the significance of this information (So What), and then you suggest what your audience might do given their new knowledge (Now What). This structure helps with small talk precisely because it's general and versatile—you can use it in a wide variety of contexts and environments to help focus and clarify your remarks. Also, its final plank lends itself to asking questions of your small-talk partner, which as we'll see will help us to project empathy and interest in our partner. Since we've already covered this conversational formula in chapter 5, I won't spend too much time here explaining how it works. Let's focus instead on how we might best apply it in chitchat.

Deploying *What–So What–Now What* can help us in two ways. First, if we seek to initiate or continue a conversation, we can simply ask these three questions to give the other person an invitation to speak. For example, we might say, "So, what did you think of the keynote speaker this morning?" (What) After the other person responds, we could follow up with another question: "How do you think the speaker's ideas will help in the short term?" (So What) The conversation after either of these questions might veer off into unexpected and interesting directions, and we might leave *What–So What–Now What* behind. But if we detect the energy in the conversation dissipating, we could come back with our third question: "Do you plan to go to the meet-and-greet the speaker is holding later?" (Now What)

What–So What–Now What can also help if others initiate a conversation with us and we wish to move the dialogue forward. Let's say we go to a convention for hikers and other outdoor enthusiasts and as part of the event there is a mixer. Someone comes up to us and asks what brought us there. We can respond, "Well, I have been an avid hiker for years [What]. I'm really excited to learn about the new equipment and tools they've got here, since I'm looking for ways to avoid getting injured and hiking farther [So What]. Do you do a lot of outdoor activities [Now What]?"

As helpful as *What–So What–Now What* might be to begin a conversation, it isn't always enough to allow us to shine during small talk. To become masters of chatter, we must pay more attention to our minute-to-minute roles as listeners and speakers. If you think about it, small talk is really just a conversation in which participants take turns speaking. We can break down this conversation further, noting the series of turn-takings that occur as participants wend their way through a series of topics.[2] To perform well in spontaneous small-talk situations, we must strive to maximize each of our turns at speaking. And the best way to do that is to deploy what I call the First Commandment of Small Talk, which is . . .

Make It about Them, Not You

So often, we presume we must come across as witty and interesting to others—that we must command the room. As a result, we tend to overplay our hands, dominating the conversation and spending too much time talking about ourselves. Although most people might want to learn about us, they're probably even more interested in talking about themselves and *feeling heard and understood by us*. When we make the conversation about us, we deny them the opportunity to feel heard and understood. We come across as self-absorbed, unempathetic, arrogant, and perhaps a bit clueless. Not the impression most of us want to leave.

At every turn we take, we have a chance to make the conversation about the other person as opposed to ourselves. Scholars distinguish between responses that *support* what another person is saying and those that *shift* the conversation back to you.[3] If your friend complains about their annoying upstairs neighbor, you might say, "Yeah, you wouldn't believe what my neighbor's been putting me through. His party last night didn't break up until after three a.m." You've just shifted the conversation back to you and your concerns rather than inviting your small-talk partner to contribute even more. A support response might be to empathize with your friend and ask for more detail about their neighbor's bad behavior and how your friend handled it.

Some usage of shift responses is fine—others do want to learn about us, and we also don't want to come across as too withdrawn, deflecting, or secretive. But so many of us make the mistake of coming back too often with shift responses. We treat stories or comments offered by others not as opportunities to learn more from or about them, but as openings for us to talk about ourselves.

To thrive in small-talk situations, focus more on delivering support responses.

As professional matchmaker and communication consultant Rachel Greenwald notes, there are many ways of doing this when it becomes our turn to speak. After our conversation partner contributes a thought or anecdote, we can say something like, "What excited you about that?" or "Wow, what happened next?" or "How did you feel when that happened?" Comments like these give your partner permission to expand on what they said or provide deeper insight and disclosure. The more you orient yourself to supporting what someone else is saying rather than shifting the focus to your own similar experience, the easier and more natural this becomes.[4]

My mother-in-law had a black belt in small talk: She loved informal conversations with others and was great at them. She relied heavily on "Tell me more . . . ," and it made quite a profound impression on me. Most members of my immediate family weren't so great at taking turns and actively listening during conversations. We all spoke at once without listening to each other. Whoever spoke loudest and longest was heard; the others weren't. Imagine how striking it was to see my mother-in-law willingly cede the floor, giving permission to the other person to speak by saying, "Tell me more." It seemed like such a generous, empathic act. I sensed immediately how much connection she forged by those three simple words, and I saw how much she learned from the people with whom she conversed. I knew that I wanted to follow her lead.

A focus on making the conversation about them and not you also helps us with two special turns that occur in conversation: initiating and exiting. To initiate a small-talk conversation, avoid being generic or using a banal start such as "How are you?" or "What do you do?" Instead, approach the initiation of a conversation as an opportunity to show curiosity about the other person and their perspective. Questions about the situation or surroundings can work well, such as "Have you ever seen so many people in blue shirts before?" or "What do you think about the number of windows in this building?" The goal is to build rapport and connection from the start, and to do so by conveying interest in the other person or your shared experience in the moment. If you're entering a situation in which you anticipate engaging in small talk, you can think of a couple of ways to kick off a conversation while projecting warmth and curiosity prior to entering the event.

If you're the recipient of a common small-talk starting question, take care not to respond too quickly with a heuristic, since that could lead to what some have called the "How are you?" loop. (One person asks, "How are you?" and the other responds, "I'm good. How are you?" Not the most fascinating conversation.) Instead, try to answer in an interesting or intriguing way that invites further questioning. The key is to offer just a bit of detail about you and your interests. If someone asks how you are, try responding with something like "I am great because I hit a personal best during my workout this morning." Your partner might ask a follow-up question, and if they do, you can answer it and in fairly short order ask a question of them and then follow up with supportive responses.

We can also make exiting conversations easier by trying to ensure that the other person feels appreciated. Many people try to end conversations by focusing exclusively on some need of their own They might say, "I'm sorry, I need to refill my drink" or "Excuse, me, I have to use the bathroom." As Greenwald points out, a better approach is to announce your departure and why you need to go but also exhibit curiosity by asking one final question that signals you've listened to what they've said and found conversing with them interesting. For example, "I'm going to check out the buffet in a minute, but I've loved chatting with you and just have one last question about that trip to Marrakesh you described. What was your favorite restaurant there, in case I get a chance to visit one day?"[5]

Greenwald calls this the "white flag approach." In auto racing, the grand marshal waves a white flag to designate the race's final lap. We can do something similar when we engage in small talk by making a graceful exit which leaves our conversation partner feeling listened to and appreciated. My mother-in-law would graciously and gracefully end her chitchat by saying something along the lines of "Thank you for telling me so much that I didn't know. I learned a lot from you. I have one more question for you before I need to go . . ."

Let's say you're at a professional function and have found yourself in a conversation with someone about a recent move. You might say, "I'd like to know a bit more about why you chose to move to that part of town." Upon hearing your partner's response, you might end by saying, "Your choice makes a lot of sense. I need to reconnect with some colleagues over there. Thanks for giving me the scoop and it was a pleasure to chat with you."

Refine Your Remarks

What–So What–Now What and the First Commandment of Small Talk are the fundamentals of chitchat. As we practice and master them, we can improve our performance further by paying attention to the following tips:

Tip #1: Seek Comparable Levels of Self-Disclosure
As important as it is to make the conversation about the other person, it does, of course, still need to include information about ourselves. Greenwald suggests aiming for a three-to-one ratio of support versus shift responses. In asking questions of others, we should be sure to provide meaningful and informative answers about our own lives when asked.

We also shouldn't shrink from touching on some of our deeper feelings or concerns. We might fear that strangers or acquaintances will find self-disclosure on our part awkward, but as research shows, deeper conversations yield a more gratifying experience and more connectedness among participants than more superficial talk does.

Further, people tend to find conversations most satisfying when they entail a relatively balanced, two-way exchange of information. Don't treat small talk as a stand-in for your weekly therapy session, but don't put all of the emphasis on the other person, either, and remain a closed book to them or make them feel like they're being interrogated. People want to learn about you *and* know that you are listening empathetically to them.

Tip #2: Avoid Putting Your Partner on the Spot
As I've suggested, making the conversation about the other person will usually entail posing questions of others. But we must take care to do so in ways that don't put them on the spot or antagonize them. Posing questions directly (for example, "How long have you worked at your current company?") can give your small-talk partner the feeling of being interrogated by a potential boss in a job interview. Instead, ask open-ended questions that might lead to conversation about a positive topic, something like "What do you enjoy doing when you're not here?"

In posing open-ended questions, we relinquish some measure of control—we don't know where our partner is going to take the conversation. But that's precisely why open-ended questions are so important. We're giving our partner the opportunity to co-create the conversation with us. And as I think you'll find, a co-created conversation is usually a better one for all involved.

Particularly in a group of people you don't know well, it's important to read the room and tailor what you say until you have a clear sense of your conversation partner's personality. For instance, although you might enjoy sarcasm and see it as a form of humor, not everyone does. Start more softly and warmly with your small-talk partner, especially in the early stages of a conversation when you're just getting to know them. If something they say signals to you that they'll appreciate sarcasm or a snarky remark, then you might move in that direction, but tread carefully and pay close attention to whether your tone is being reciprocated.

A negative comment on your part risks boomeranging and reflecting poorly on you. If you're trying to build rapport and project warmth and empathy, negativity belies that image. If you deem snarkiness appropriate for the conversation, choose to be gently self-deprecating. It's certainly safer, and others tend to find it endearing. Comedians often win audiences over with self-deprecating humor, and so can you. Rather than saying, "I can't believe it took the kitchen so long for food that tastes this bad," you might say, "I'm glad I'm not the only one who struggles to make a good pasta sauce."

Tip #3: Be a Team Player

Too often, we tend to approach small talk as a competition between ourselves and the other person. Our opponent is lobbing shots over the net at us, and we're trying to send the ball back the other way before it bounces twice. Both of us are trying to win the Most Interesting Person in the Room Award. It's like a zero-sum game—only one of us can "win," and we had best look out for ourselves. But there's another way to look at small talk: as a team sport in which we're all working together to obtain a positive result. This is the "small talk as hacky-sack" philosophy: we're all just trying to keep the ball aloft, and when it drops, all of us lose.

As you can imagine, this second approach is more conducive to building relationships with others. It's also less stressful and more fun for us, as we no longer feel so lonely and pressured to "win." But if small talk is a team sport, we have to do our part. As we go back and forth taking turns, we should focus on making life easier for our partners by setting them up to succeed in their next turn. To the extent we can, we should try to point to transitions between topics and remind our partners of the broader logic and history of the conversation.

One way to accomplish this task is by starting off a comment of ours by paraphrasing what we heard from our partner. For example, if you're speaking to someone who is a newcomer to your city and who has spent a moment or two describing how much they love it, you might say something like "I'm glad to hear that you like it in this city after moving in from Baltimore. I'm wondering, what about this city most surprised you when you first arrived?" We can also end our comments with a question that likewise serves to help transition between topics or ideas. If we've been talking about our recent success landing a new client, we might say, "Well, I've told you my good news. What's the best thing that's happened to you in the last week, either professionally or personally?"

Tip #4: Avoid Swiping Left Too Soon
In our era of multitasking and overwhelming choice, we can sometimes find it hard to concentrate on a small-talk conversation for very long. We might glance across the room and feel pangs of FOMO, wondering if we might have an even better or more productive time chatting with someone else. Giving in to these feelings, we might extract ourselves from conversations too quickly, causing offense to others. Bailing opportunistically on conversations in progress might also cost us in terms of connections we might have made or new knowledge we might have gained.

I'm as guilty as anyone of "swiping left" too quickly. My greatest small-talk weakness is my failure to be fully present in conversations. I'm often distractedly scanning the room, worrying that I'm missing an opportunity to have an even better conversation with someone else. I find myself rushing through structured responses and then muttering a perfunctory excuse as I tear myself away from the conversation. When I do this too frequently, I come away from events drained and uninspired. I've spent too much time flitting around, worrying about missing out, and I haven't taken enough time with any particular person to forge a meaningful connection.

If you begin to feel restless, resist the urge to swipe left on the situation. Instead, refocus yourself on being present and listening intently. Remind yourself that it can take a few minutes for people to relax enough to engage with you and say something interesting. Play a little game with yourself, challenging yourself to remember one key fact about each person you meet or inviting each person to share their thoughts about a particular topic.

Try as we might, we can't engineer small talk to maximize its productivity for us, since we can't know what we're missing if we leave a conversation too quickly to jump into another. A far better approach is simply to relax, focus, and let conversations run a more natural course, bowing out if we become tired or feel that the energy is draining from the conversation.

Tip #5: Minimize Your Chances of Offending Others by Reflecting, Questioning, and Paraphrasing

Given how polarized and heated public discourse has become, it can feel frightfully easy to step over the line, making yourself vulnerable to harsh criticism or worse. Let's remember, the goal of small talk is connection and congeniality. This doesn't mean you should bury your own views in order to keep the peace; the point is to approach each conversation as an opportunity to build rapport and find common ground with your small-talk partner.

First, as you begin a small-talk encounter, avoid making any assumptions about views that your audience may or may not hold. Before introducing or weighing in on a new topic, listen to what others are saying, gauging the substance of their ideas, the details they're bringing to bear, and their tone of voice. When you do begin to contribute, test out the waters by posing generic questions rather than coming straight out with a declaration that requires a direct reaction. Let's say you're at a friend's cocktail party, and the conversation turns political. Rather than opening with your position on a particular candidate or issue, you might listen and observe what others are saying. This allows you to gather information about your audience, and strategize an approach for sharing your views in a way that your audience will be best positioned to receive.

Paraphrasing can help here. You can keep the conversation going without injecting your beliefs by posing open questions such as "Tell me more about your thoughts on [fill in the blank]" and then paraphrasing what you hear. Doing this gives you a chance to understand why the person with whom you're conversing holds the views that they do, which will then allow you to contribute or counter in a way that lowers the emotional temperature for everyone.

Let's say that in the course of a conversation, you assert that you believe professional sports teams should change their mascots to be more politically correct, and your conversation partner vehemently disagrees. You might feel tempted to blurt out, "Wow, how can you possibly believe that? Some mascots are completely offensive!" But in reality, this response likely won't change your conversation partner's mind. Instead, you can downplay the tension and create curiosity by summarizing both views. You might say, "Just like what happens when players disagree with a referee's call, it seems we have a difference of opinion."

In-the-moment reflection, questioning, and paraphrasing can help your small talk go more smoothly and reduce your anxiety about offending or being offended. More generally, research has suggested that the more we can do to communicate our openness to engaging with opposing viewpoints, the more likely we are to connect, learn, and avoid conflict during a conversation. This makes sense: if we feel that others respect us enough to listen carefully and with an open mind to what we're saying, we're less likely to bristle at what they say. By explicitly telling people that we understand them, by pointing to common ground, by softening our claims, and by making more positive statements, we can show what researchers call "conversational receptiveness." As others let their guard down, we can engage with them more productively and enjoyably.[6] We're more likely to encourage others to sincerely consider our views when we start by making clear that we are sincerely willing to hear theirs.

Application in Action

With the First Commandment of Small Talk in mind, let's now take a look at how we might structure specific responses when it is our turn to speak.

Scenario #1
You're at a wedding in a distant city and are starting up a conversation with someone you don't know. They ask you where you are from.

A possible response:
"Well, I was originally born in Omaha, but I moved southward until settling in Houston [What]. While my move was for work, I have really enjoyed the opportunity to attend lots of

sporting events and eat really good food [So What]. So, I am
curious to know, have you ever lived in or visited Texas [Now
What]?"

In this response, we provide insight into who we are in a way that is
not banal or trivial. At the same time, rather than continue to focus all
of the attention on us, we set up our partner to contribute by posing a
question that follows logically from our response.

Scenario #2
*You're attending a national convention in your field, and you've gone to a
mixer. You're mingling with a group of strangers who all work at different companies and come from different cities.*

A possible response:
"I'm Matt Abrahams, and I'm from Silicon Valley in California
[What]. I am really excited to learn about tonight's topic be-
cause I have listened to several of the presenter's podcast ep-
isodes [So What]. What got you interested in tonight's topic
[Now What]?"

In this response, our closing question probes for common ground.
By getting others in the group to respond, we take the focus off of us.
If we want, we can expand slightly on the What and So What portions
to reveal a bit more about ourselves or our personality. For instance, we
might make a self-deprecating joke about Silicon Valley in the course
of identifying our place of residence. Or we might briefly mention a
couple of our favorite podcast episodes by the presenter. Any touch of
added detail might increase the odds that we'll trigger recognition and
a response from someone else.

Scenario #3
*We're at a family Thanksgiving gathering, and we find ourselves standing
next to our great aunt's next-door neighbor, whom we haven't met before. The
initial foray into a conversation feels awkward, and a deafening silence ensues.
You both happen to have a portion of a corn dish on your plates.*

A possible response:
"Wow, this corn dish is amazing [What]. I'm always looking for new ways to prepare it. I mean, boiling and grilling it are fine, but I appreciate a little creativity [So What]. Do you have a favorite vegetable dish, either to eat or cook [Now What]?"

In this response, we invoke a shared experience, inviting our partner to speak about a topic on which you know they're likely to have an opinion. Once they make an initial contribution, subsequent contributions might come more easily, and you might also learn additional information that triggers new questions for you to pose.

Parting Thought

During the process of gathering my thoughts for this chapter, I had an interesting experience that put these concepts into a clearer perspective. I attended a fundraising dinner for a group supporting cancer patients. Initially, the hostess sat me at a table where the small talk was simply sensational. The eight or so people at the table and I were all chatting energetically and responding in supportive ways to one another. We were talking about how cancer had touched our lives, where we lived, where our kids went to school. We were laughing, leaning in as we spoke, nodding, smiling a lot. After just thirty minutes or so, I had connected on LinkedIn with three people and made plans to have coffee with a fourth. It looked like the connections I made during the evening would last beyond this important event.

But then our hostess tapped me on the shoulder. Some guests were not showing up, and a nearby table didn't have enough people. Would I be willing to switch? I agreed, saying goodbye to my new friends and making my way to my new seat. To my disappointment, I found that the social environment at my new table was entirely different from that at my previous one. Here the guests were quiet, avoiding eye contact with one another and gazing around the room.

When one of the guests did speak, the conversation that ensued was superficial and short-lived. Guests asked banal, generic questions such as "What did you do this summer?" A response from their small-talk partner would prompt a shift response, causing the conversations to go nowhere.

Emboldened by all the thinking I was doing about small talk, I decided to put my own skills to work to help others. At one point, a guest responded to a question by noting that they took a trip to Hawaii that summer. Their partner replied, "Oh, I went to Costa Rica," a response that promised to lead to just another stunted conversation. I saw my opportunity to jump in and shake things up for the better. "Hey, you know, my wife and I honeymooned in Costa Rica, too," I said to the guest who had just spoken. "We traveled around the country and loved it, especially the cloud forest and the quetzal we saw there. What areas did you visit? What did you find most interesting?" After this guest responded, I asked several supportive questions, prompting the subject of birds to pop back up. Another guest jumped in, describing how he'd traveled to see a bald eagle.

Within just ten minutes or so, the conversation was moving. It still wasn't as lively and engaging as at the previous table, but we did have fun. People at my table were laughing and leaning in more. One person at the table asked me if they could connect with me on LinkedIn. Two others who had begun to chat exchanged contact information with one another.

My point here is not that I'm a master at small talk and you should invite me to all of your parties (we've already established that this is not true and that I have my own weaknesses to work on). Rather, I'd like to suggest what might become possible as we build up our spontaneous communication skills. With a bit of work, we can not only handle ourselves well but also begin to spread happiness, connection, and collegiality wherever we go, inspiring others to open themselves up to people around them and to learn from them. The positive benefits of small talk can be significant indeed, but only if we break from our established habits and develop a more helpful—and structured—way of engaging. So don't struggle through another social occasion. Get out there and start practicing!

Application #2

TOASTS THAT TANTALIZE
(AND TRIBUTES AND INTRODUCTIONS, TOO)

Key Insight

Toasts, tributes, and introductions are some of the most common instances of spontaneous speaking out there. Whether it's at product launches, panels, weddings, quinceañeras, funerals, or luncheons, we often must speak up to mark life events, celebrate accomplishments, and introduce others. Almost reflexively, most of us focus in the moment on how others are perceiving us. Yet, these situations aren't about us at all. The whole point of these public moments is to say something meaningful about others, whether they're individuals, teams, or organizations.

To help break our habit of focusing on our own worries and needs, we can think of toasts, tributes, and introductions as gifts we bestow on our audience and the people or groups we are acknowledging. Just as we consider what kinds of tangible gifts people might like, want, or need, something similar holds for our spoken gifts. Our focus on our recipients leads us to consider the best way to package our gift, and that in turn prompts us to think about structure. After all, we want others to access our gifts without much effort. We want them to enjoy our verbal offerings and to remember them. By deploying a structure, we can make our toasts, tributes, and introductions more focused, clear, and concise, so that those we're acknowledging enjoy what they're hearing and feel like they've gotten their due.

Why It Matters

Celebratory comments often feel obligatory or even a necessary evil, but they actually can serve an array of important functions. In the course of honoring and recognizing a person, team, or organization that matters to us, we can demonstrate the respect, caring, sense of connection, and understanding we have for them. We also can set the tone for the larger event at which we're speaking, focusing the audience and calibrating their expectations for other speakers who might follow us. We can build closer bonds with honorees while enhancing our audience's sense of collegiality and immediacy. And with a structure to fall back on, these occasions may turn out to be less daunting than we presume.

Craft Your Content

A useful structure to invoke if someone asks you to offer up celebratory or commemorative remarks is a four-part formula that I call WHAT:

- **W Why are we here:** First, identify the context for the gathering. For instance, we might have convened to celebrate the life of the deceased, to honor a team's strong efforts, and so on.
- **H How are you connected:** Let the audience know who you are and why you are speaking.
- **A Anecdotes or learnings:** Offer the audience some stories and/or lessons you learned that relate to the person, group, or event you're commemorating. Make these stories or lessons relatable, appropriate, and concise.
- **T Thank:** Express gratitude and offer well-wishes to the person, group, or event that you're commemorating.

Let's take a closer look at each of these steps.

Step #1: Why Are We Here

Clarify the purpose of the event as you see it. Doing so helps others focus and sets expectations for what is to come. Defining the event for your audience also allows you to express emotion, convey the event's importance, and begin to celebrate the subjects of your communication.

Examples:

"Because of her many professional accomplishments, I am super excited to hear Shandra speak today about the entertainment business and her inspiring career as a recording artist who is also on the Broadway stage."

"This wedding brings together two of the most caring and special people I know."

Step #2: How Are You Connected

Often, some of your listeners won't know who you are or what your role in the event is. Take a moment to share the nature of your relationship to those whom you're commemorating. Doing so can also allow you to slip in some background information about the subject of your talk and perhaps even a bit of humor.

Examples:

"Shandra and I studied voice together at Juilliard for six pivotal months and eventually recorded our first album together way back in 1994."

"Not only have I known both of the soon-to-be newlyweds for over a decade, but I was the one who introduced them at, of all places, a *Star Trek* convention. Who knew that a Klingon and a Romulan would fall in love and get married?"

Step #3: Anecdotes or Learnings

Now you share the bulk of your engaging content, including humor, emotion, and lessons learned. In line with advice given earlier in this book, make sure your stories have structure, are appropriate, have a clear point, and aren't too long. When it comes to length, think a few minutes, not tens of minutes.

Examples:

"I am continuously amazed at how Shandra can take a jazz standard that we've all heard a hundred times before and breathe new life into it. I've learned many things from her, but perhaps the most important is how a great song sung from the heart and with real intelligence can instantly transport you."

"The first time these two met they each asked me separately to interrupt their conversation about how many tribbles can fit on the starship *Enterprise* so they could go home early. Although they're both die-hard Trekkies, they were not having a good time. It is a good thing I ignored them both!"

Step #4: Thank

Conclude by expressing gratitude to the audience and/or to those you're commemorating. Again, you might find an opportunity to slip in additional background information about those whom you're commemorating.

Examples:

"I want to thank Shandra for being a great collaborator and friend. I know you will learn a lot from her. Please welcome two-time Grammy Award winner Shandra Delacorte to the stage."

"Thank you for being such amazing friends to me and all of us here. We all wish you the best as you 'boldly go' into this new phase of your relationship and life."

Refine Your Remarks

We've all suffered through bad toasts, tributes, and introductions. Not only can they dampen the mood; they also can denigrate and damage the reputation of everyone involved. We can't always anticipate how others will receive what we say. Still, by leveraging the following guidelines, we can improve the odds that our comments will have the positive impact we desire.

Tip #1: Be Brief and to the Point

Long toasts, tributes, or introductions are usually bad ones. Trying to cover too many topics reduces the impact of your remarks. When you are one of many speakers, think about your remarks in the context of the event as a whole. The audience will become restless if each speaker takes up too much time, gives remarks that feel unfocused or too broad, or repeats the same material. I have yet to hear someone complain that a commemoration of someone else was too short. Share only enough information to appropriately honor those involved, given the context in which you're speaking. A good tribute succinctly and memorably acknowledges what makes the subject of the tribute special—and that's *all* it does.

Tip #2: Prepare to Be Emotional

In many cases, toasts, tributes, and introductions elicit strong emotions, both positive (in the case of weddings, graduations, bar mitzvahs, or quinceañeras) and negative (divorces, funerals, retirements). Consider how you might respond in these situations if your emotions begin to flow. If you anticipate losing control, make a plan ahead of time with someone who might step in should you need them. Alternatively, be prepared yourself to jump to a closing line so you can step aside. While tempting, reading from notes on paper or a phone can often make things worse when you are highly emotional. It is easy to get distracted and it can cause you to disconnect from your audience.

Think, too, about your audience's emotional state and tailor your remarks to them as best you can. If you're at a wedding and you're expected to channel love for the newly betrothed, will other emotions peek through in a story you might think to tell? Similarly, is now the time to chime in with some salty humor that might turn off some audience members? Be mindful about appropriate ways you might express emotion publicly given your relationship to the person or people being celebrated and the breadth of guests who will be in attendance. Audiences at a corporate event celebrating a product launch will usually expect a project manager to show more emotion than a senior leader. After all, the project manager was much more intimately involved with the team that did the work. A senior leader who seemed overly moved might come across as inauthentic or even a bit odd. Reflect for a quick moment on what you mean to the person being celebrated, and what audiences expect you to mean to them. Be sure to stay in bounds.

Tip #3: Be Vigilant about Shining the Spotlight Away from You
When you're telling a story about the person you're commemorating, keep details about yourself and your own involvement to a minimum. Refrain from saying too much about what you think. A good way to assess how you are doing in this respect is to notice whether you're using the word "I" a lot in your remarks. If you are, then see if you might return the focus to the subject of your communication.

Tip #4: Make Your Anecdotes Accessible and Appropriate
No one likes to feel left out. Avoid stories that only a few people in the audience will understand and appreciate. Make sure the content of your stories and any curse words you use are appropriate for your audience. If you feel it necessary or desirable to use a piece of jargon or an acronym, briefly explain the term to your audience by way of background.

Tip #5: Strive for Unity
The world is increasingly polarized, and many people hold passionate views. Since you likely seek to forge deeper relationships and connections, public remarks meant to honor another person or group are a time to seek out common ground. Offer commentary that everyone in your audience can support, without compromising your own values. This might seem challenging, but it's my experience that middle ground almost always exists when you search earnestly for it.

Suppose you find yourself celebrating a team's successful merger. If this team is led by a manager whose approach and political beliefs run counter to yours, you can focus on how this team reflected your corporate values rather than the manager's personal ones. This speech might not be the right opportunity to needle that manager for their approach or beliefs. If you simply cannot avoid it or would feel disingenuous giving a speech that did not address the differences, then perhaps you should suggest that someone else give the remarks. But if you can, use this opportunity to create a bridge to discuss the corporate values and priorities you want to see adopted by the newly merged team. This might, in turn, create an opening for a more intimate and honest conversation with this manager or team down the line.

Tip #6: Set Others Up for Success
Think of yourself as the opening act for whoever follows you (the next speaker, the person you introduce, and so forth). Try your best to set them up for success. I often refer to this as "clearing the runway" so those who follow you can enjoy a smooth and timely takeoff. Provide logistics, agenda, and "housekeeping" information. End your comments on a positive note, leaving people engaged and excited for what is next. Imagine how *you* would like someone to introduce you, and do the same. You might say, in advance of formally introducing the next speaker, "Juana has lots of interesting things to say. Before I introduce her, I wanted to let you know that we will be providing notes of what she discusses after the talk and we'll have some drinks and light snacks in the bar area tonight after we conclude."

Application in Action

Toasts, tributes, and introductions can vary depending on a number of factors, such as whether the person you're commemorating has authority over you, whether you're at a professional or personal event, and whether what you're commemorating is a happy or sad occasion. The following scenarios suggest how you might put the WHAT formula to good use:

Scenario #1
You're addressing your team of about a dozen people, introducing them to two senior leaders from the corporate office.

A possible response:
"Sy and Jeanne have flown in to spend some time with our team [W]. I have worked for them over the past three years and am excited for us to get some time with both of them in

person [H]. The last time Sy and Jeanne were here, we were able to review our plans for the quarter and prioritize our efforts. This time, they hope to see our progress and share some ideas from the home office [A]. Sy and Jeanne, we really appreciate you making the time to visit [T]."

This introduction not only provides context; it also sets expectations for the importance and quality of the interactions to come.

Scenario #2

Your team has notched an amazing success, and you want to take a moment to celebrate it with team members.

A possible response:

"Wow! We just closed the last deal of the quarter three days early [W]. I have been behind the scenes watching how each of you went above and beyond to get this deal done [H]. I remember back to three months ago when we first learned of this opportunity and selected each of you to join the team because we believed you could complete this deal [A]. I and the other executives want to compliment you on your creativity and tenacity in bringing this deal to a close. Thank you [T]."

Here, as an added bonus, the speaker highlights the teamwork and approach that she would like to see repeated in the future.

Scenario #3

A colleague of yours has reached her five-year work anniversary, and it's your turn to acknowledge her.

A possible response:

"Ting, congratulations on being at the company for five years [W]. We have worked together on a number of projects, and I have learned a lot from you [H]. I remember the time when we ordered all of the T-shirts for our conference, and they came in the wrong sizes and colors. You remained amazingly calm and collected while I was running around crazed [A]. Ting, thanks for being a great colleague, mentor, and friend [T]. Happy anniversary."

In this example, we highlight the strengths of the person being celebrated while telling a detailed, self-deprecating story.

Parting Thought

Not long ago, a dear colleague of mine passed away of cancer. Her death had been fairly swift, and the news of it came as a shock. Edwina was influential at the community college where I used to teach, and many people turned to her for guidance and sage advice. She had mentored me for years, and I looked to her as a source of positive energy and wisdom in my life. Hearing that she had passed away, I was deeply sad and felt the urge to commemorate her in some meaningful way.

I got my chance a few days later when colleagues who knew Edwina convened informally via Zoom to remember her. Each of us took turns expressing our feelings and recounting memories of Edwina; none of us had prepared our remarks in advance. Because so many of us showed up, we agreed to keep our comments brief—just a minute or so each. The mood was somber, although a couple of us took the opportunity to recall some lighter memories and reflections. When it came time for me to speak, I hoped to say something that conveyed my deep respect and admiration of Edwina, without running on too long or burdening others with too much emotion.

Mobilizing the WHAT structure, I wound up saying something like the following:

Edwina was an amazing person whose wise council was sought after far and wide [W]. I was fortunate enough to follow Edwina in two leadership roles she held [H]. I clearly remember being part of some heated decision-making sessions where I, as many of you likely still do, thought to myself: "What would Edwina do?" Reflecting on her demeanor and approach helped me to make useful contributions in these situations [A]. I invite all of us to remember Edwina for how she touched our lives and the many, many other lives with whom she had contact [T].

Although my remarks were brief, they allowed me to say something meaningful without hogging the floor. Rather than falling back on clichés or platitudes, I managed to convey something about Edwina that mattered to me (I really do think of her all the time when I'm in tough spots, recalling her words of wisdom and ways of approaching life). The anecdote I gave was appropriate given that the audience was a mix of close colleagues, direct reports, and supervisors, and my message set others up for success by inviting them to share their own thoughts about how Edwina had impacted us.

Having a structure to fall back on wasn't make-or-break in this situation—I probably would have done okay without it. But a structure did help me stay focused and prevent my emotions from distracting me. I hope you'll find success with the WHAT structure, and that you'll also start to think of commemorating others as a gift you give rather than a burdensome chore. Life is short, and when it comes down to it, the gifts of meaning that we give are among the most important and satisfying, not just for others, but also for ourselves.

Application #3

MAKE THAT (IM)PERFECT PITCH

Key Insight

When engaging spontaneously with others, we often hope to do more than simply inform them of our thoughts, ideas, and opinions. We want to *convince* them to see the world as we do or to act in a way we believe is best for them. We may want colleagues to agree with our ideas, our customers to buy products we're selling, our love interests to agree to go out with us on first dates, our children to modify their behavior and respect our rules, and our neighbors to keep their dogs off our lawns. Books have been written about how to communicate more persuasively, and I heartily recommend that you read them.[1] But to become more persuasive, we must also understand how to wield influence *in the moment.*

It is one thing to prepare a stellar speech ahead of time; it is another to be able to adapt our pitches on the fly to reflect what we're discovering about our audiences and their needs. Thorough preparation can help us anticipate what will move our audience, but we must be able to listen in the moment, read the cues we're receiving, and respond to our audience's needs in ways that feel authentic. Having a structure to fall back on frees us to pay more attention and adjust in real time. A structure can also help to ensure that our spontaneous pitch is logical and consistent with what we're learning about others and their needs.

Why It Matters

If we attend to how we pitch others in the moment, we'll respond more closely to others' needs. They in turn will perceive us as more credible, authentic, and empathetic, and they'll regard our messaging as more relevant. We'll stand a better chance of winning their full support and favor.

Craft Your Content

To land a strong pitch that responds to your audience's needs, try a structure I discussed in chapter 5 called *Problem–Solution–Benefit.*

> **Problem:** First, define a challenge, issue, or pain point that you are addressing, one that your audience shares.
> **Solution:** Second, present a fix to the problem, spelling out the specific steps, process/product, or method for remedying the problem.
> **Benefit:** Finally, describe the advantages and gains that adoption of your proposed solution will yield.

As I think you'll find, this structure works well in a wide array of situations when you're trying to convince others. Here is a bit more detail on these three steps.

Step #1: State the Problem Concretely

As clearly and concisely as you can, provide a direct account of the issue at hand in terms that your audience will appreciate. Sometimes you might find it possible to frame the problem in a positive way, as an opportunity to improve a current situation or undertake a new venture. Other times, you can convey the problem more directly as an unfortunate situation or pain point that requires attention. You can prepare by researching the types of presentations that have succeeded with your audiences in the past.

Examples:

If you want friends at a dinner party to support your point of view about the need to tackle homelessness in your city, you might say, "This problem is rampant in our city, as seen recently in the news."

If you want colleagues at work to adopt a new behavior, you might say, "Aren't you tired of being underappreciated and disconnected from what others on the team are doing?"

In defining the problem or opportunity, think about what kind of evidence will likely resonate most with your audience. For example, if you know your audience cares about data, provide statistics that support your claim. If your audience tends to favor specific examples, tell relevant stories and anecdotes or provide a demonstration. Some audiences might like you to take a direct, hard-hitting approach to defining a problem. Others might want you to be a bit softer, perhaps using a touch of humor when introducing an issue. As discussed in chapter 6, it's important to create common ground with your audience, and you can do that by reflecting on some basic questions: Will most audience members be familiar with the problem I want to discuss, or will it be new to them? What personal connection might they have to my topic? By sprinkling in a bit of background, using familiar terms, or referencing a personal connection, you can make the problem you define seem more relevant.

In the course of presenting the problem, you might also point to the challenges that have prevented people from addressing it. When pitching Tesla's Powerwall battery, Elon Musk didn't simply evoke a problem—out-of-control global warming fostered by fossil fuel emissions. He also pointed to the barriers that currently prevent humanity from transitioning to solar power: variations in energy production, which give rise to the need for batteries; poor existing battery technology; and so on. Taking this extra step of portraying the specific challenges that prevent a solution can make the problem seem more difficult, and the solution you provide (which will of course surmount these challenges) all the more compelling.[2]

Step #2: Detail the Solution

Introduce a solution that appears feasible and reasonable given the problem or opportunity under discussion. Referring back to chapter 6, communicate your solution in a way that a given audience will find focused and accessible. If your solution is more complex, itemize the parts of it so people can clearly understand it.

> **Examples:**
>
> "Policy approaches modeled after our current programs tend to partner city officials with local businesses. Adopting these will allow us to find more job opportunities for unhoused people, allowing them to get back on their feet."
>
> "Create dashboards that show progress against your goals. Sharing those in advance of our weekly meeting will demonstrate your work's value to the broader team."

Step #3: Lay Out the Benefits

Specify and rank the benefits that your solution will yield, beginning with the biggest, highest-value benefits and proceeding from there.

> **Examples:**
>
> "By developing a deeper understanding of the homelessness issue and fostering grassroots connections between business and government, we will not only get more people the shelter and support they need; we'll also align the community and get more people working together."
>
> "Showing your value will not only connect you more to the team; it will increase the relevance of your work and potentially help you attain the promotion you desire."

You can adjust the order of these elements if you anticipate strong resistance to your solution, or if you think your audience might balk at how you are envisioning the problem. In these cases, it may be stronger to place the benefit before the problem. A response you could give in the moment might look something like this: "What would it be like if we could increase our sales while reducing production costs [Benefit]? Our reliance on one supplier prevents us from achieving these benefits [Problem]. If we outsource our needs to two suppliers, we can easily and quickly achieve our sales and cost efficiency goals [Solution]."

• • •

Bonus Structure

That's right, there's more! If you're pitching to obtain support from others for a new or growing business venture, you might proceed by completing the following sentence starters:

- "What if you could . . ."
- "So that . . ."
- "For example . . ."
- "And that's not all . . ."

Example:

"**What if you could** intake customer orders more efficiently while offering a more personalized experience? **So that** your customers could receive their goods more quickly and you get paid faster. **For example**, using our platform, Company XYZ is now processing orders 50 percent faster and getting paid one week earlier while their customers report higher satisfaction. **And that's not all** . . . with the data we collect and analyze, we can better provide recommendations to your customers, which will increase the products they purchase from you."

• • •

Refine Your Remarks

Making use of the *Problem–Solution–Benefit* structure can really help you to shift your audience to your point of view. To further increase the odds of success, consider doing the following:

Tip #1: Use Analogies

Analogies or comparisons can help your audience understand the different elements of this structure. You might compare the significance or impact of the problem/opportunity you are defining to a previous situation that people already know. In a business setting, for instance, you might say something like, "Our current supply chain problem parallels the challenges we had with our other product line" or "Transitioning to cloud from on-premises offerings feels similar to what happened when the industry went from desktop computers to mobile devices."

Likewise, you might compare the solution you're advocating to a successful solution in another domain. If you're a health care worker trying to convince someone to eat fewer carbs, you might say, "Reducing your carbohydrate consumption is like when you cut back on your weekday wine drinking a few years back." You can also find analogues for the benefits you state. If you're speaking with a colleague at a tech company, you might say, "Atlassian saw a tenfold improvement in response time scores when they implemented a similar solution."

Tip #2: Offer Consistent Solutions

If you can show that your proposed solution is consistent with prior actions or ways of addressing an issue, your audience will be more likely to buy in. In sales, this is called the "foot in the door" technique.[3] We like to feel as if we're acting consistently and to have others perceive that we are as well. We also will more likely agree to something if we can spot some precedent for it. If you're arguing that the government should cut taxes to spur economic growth, note that the government has done so successfully to grapple with previous economic downturns. If you're arguing that you deserve a raise or promotion, point to other people who have received one after performances comparable to yours. Showing that your solution fits with previous ones makes saying yes feel like more of a foregone conclusion.

Tip #3: Frame Benefits in Positive Terms[4]

Phrasing matters. Think of positive ways you can convey a benefit and you'll have an easier time convincing your audience. If a given solution has worked 75 percent of the time, we can point that out instead of saying that it has a 25 percent failure rate. Most people would be more excited to learn about a solution that worked three-quarters of the time. We discussed in chapter 6 the value of piquing your audience's curiosity by adding tension into your discussion. If you take that approach, it's especially important to be ready to frame a solution in positive terms to ensure that you are resolving the tension of the problem.

Relatedly, try to frame solutions in ways that highlight what people have to gain. According to the popular theory of loss aversion, we naturally are more inclined to avoid risk and bad stuff from happening—sometimes even sacrificing more in order to achieve something good. If you evoke risk by suggesting what people stand to lose, you might unwittingly turn them off to a potential solution more than you would otherwise.

One of my favorite examples here has to do with selling cars. Sure, you could describe a given car as "used" in the course of pointing to its features and benefits, but that would incline your audience to think about the potential drawbacks of used cars—their unreliability, the high cost of repairs, and so on. Far better if you called the car "previously enjoyed." It's a subtle difference, but this latter phrasing probably won't evoke as much risk in your audience's mind. On the contrary, it suggests that the car has a long history of being enjoyed, and that your audience will enjoy it, too.

Tip #4: Address the Obstacles
Many people want to eat more fruits and vegetables and fewer fatty and sweet foods. They know such dietary changes are good for them. They know more healthy eating will help them to lose weight, feel better, lower their blood pressure, and achieve other health goals. They might have every intention of changing their diets for the better. They might be pumped up to do so.

But then they run up against some obstacles. Maybe they live in a food desert where fruits and vegetables are hard to come by. Maybe they travel a lot and frequently find themselves with few healthy food options. Despite their best efforts, these obstacles might prevent them from changing their behavior, even if they want to. They find themselves subsisting on burgers, fries, and soda, just as they long have.

When we try to influence others, we often focus exclusively on the benefits of our solution. As important as those benefits are, we must also pay at least some attention to barriers that might prevent people from thinking or doing what we want. If we don't, we might lose our credibility with the audience. Imagine how frustrating it might be to have someone convince you of how great a course of action is, and yet fail to address the very real challenges you face in embracing it. They're dangling something attractive in front of you, yet not helping you access it. Pretty insensitive on their part. And not fun for you.

We must do our best to make our requests of others—our solutions—practical as well as attractive. Sometimes that means dropping a few ideas as to how they might resolve obstacles in their path. Other times that might mean framing our solutions in ways that take into account the barriers others face. If you're trying to persuade someone to play tennis with you, and you know they must parent their kids during the weekends while their partner works, you might suggest a tennis date during a weekday evening rather than mentioning the possibility of playing on the weekends. If you're trying to sell someone a product but know they have a limited budget, you might offer up a pay-as-you-go approach as your solution. Alternatively, you might address the sticker shock directly by sharing that other products end up costing more down the line, but yours will last longer and be cheaper overall.

We can't simply promote the changes we want to see. We stand a far better chance of succeeding if we take empathy to a new level, considering as well what might prevent others from buying into those changes, and addressing those concerns as part of our messaging.[5]

Tip #5: Tone Down the Perfectionism
When we're trying to influence others in a spontaneous situation, we often feel that what we say must be perfect. As we've seen earlier throughout this book, the drive for perfection can in turn make us overly stiff and self-conscious—we become terrified of saying the wrong thing.

When it comes to pitching ideas, a bit of imperfection is a *good* thing. As marketing professor Baba Shiv explains, highly polished presentations tend to invite criticism—audiences want to find flaws in what they hear. People are inherently skeptical when listening to others' ideas. They feel protective of their existing beliefs and attitudes and fear adopting new ones. In many instances, they also like to feel as if their own perspectives are being validated. They want to feel like they are adding value, and offering up criticism or suggestions is a powerful way of doing that.

Shiv references an old saying in Silicon Valley: If you're an entrepreneur approaching an investor for funding, "you're only going to get advice. If you go for advice [because your idea is still imperfect], you're going to get money." He describes some lore from the world of advertising in which an executive pitches an ad campaign to a client but fails because the campaign is too perfect. His boss offers him some advice: give one of the people in the visual ad campaign too much hair on their arm. That way, the client can agree to the campaign but also has the opportunity to add an opinion of their own—lose the hair. By creating opportunities for others to contribute and collaborate, you can increase your potential influence and buy-in.

The take-home message is that a little perfection is a good thing. Too much of it can backfire.

Application in Action

Can *Problem–Solution–Benefit* really work in a wide variety of circumstances that we might encounter? Absolutely. Consider the following three scenarios, which span both professional and personal life. Each one comes with just a bit of analysis as to how the suggested response might work to our benefit.

Scenario #1
You're interviewing someone for a job, trying to convince them to come to your company.

A possible response:
"You will not only hone your skills in project management, but you will have access and influence with senior management [Benefit]. This job will have you defining and implementing our go-to-market plan, which means you will have a big impact

169

inside and outside our firm [Opportunity]. I and the people you interviewed with hope you choose to work as part of our team [Solution]."

In this case, we lead with the benefits. By doing so, we frame the choice in terms of what the person has to gain, nudging them away from thinking about potential losses at a different job where they may not have the same access. Focusing on both a skills benefit and an interpersonal benefit helps reinforce that this is a good job.

Scenario #2
You want to get someone to do you a favor.

A possible response:
"I need to rearrange two large bookcases, since that would allow my office's new area rug to fit and allow for a clearer view to my big-screen TV [Problem]. Since I helped you move your new sofa up your stairs, I was hoping you could come over tonight to return the favor by helping me move these bookcases [Solution]. We can then better enjoy watching the game and have a drink [Benefit]."

Here, reminding the other person of reciprocity can increase compliance. Similarly, focusing on how the "victim" benefits immediately will likely increase compliance.

Scenario #3
You're going out for dinner with your significant other, and you want to convince them that your choice of restaurant is the right one.

A possible response:
"While I know you suggested we go for Italian food, I hear that the menu at the Chinese restaurant just changed and that their chef just received a prestigious award [Opportunity]. What if we go to the Chinese restaurant tonight and make Italian food during the week [Solution]? This way we can try

out the new Chinese menu, and by cooking Italian at home, we can be guaranteed to have lots of leftovers which means we save money on lunches [Benefit]."

In this example, acknowledging the other's point of view makes you seem more reasonable and empathetic. It makes clear that you're listening to and registering the other person's desires and concerns and not simply trying to bully or steamroll your way toward your desired goal. Framing the benefit as a long-term win for the other can help, too.

Parting Thought

I've always been fascinated by how deftly children deploy effective persuasion in the moment. When my older son was twelve, he asked whether my wife and I might buy him an expensive electric guitar. At the time, his closet was full of partially used toys and equipment. I couldn't see indulging this hobby only to see him drop it, so I said no. What ensued was a spontaneous pitch that was quite impeccably structured.

"Dad," he said, "aren't you and Mom always encouraging me to be more creative and keep myself busy?" With this opener, he articulated an opportunity available to both him and us. Next, he offered up a solution: "If you buy me this guitar, I can teach myself to read music and practice in my room." Finally came a benefit, both to him and us: "The first song I will learn to play is one of your favorite Carlos Santana songs, and my friend told me that learning to play the guitar helped him understand math better in school."

My wife and I were quite impressed with this persuasive plea, and we granted his wish. We were even more impressed just a few weeks later when he played some cool music on his new guitar. The key to my son's persuasive success was his ability to address our concerns in a clear, succinct, logical way. Your pitches can succeed as well. By leveraging persuasive frameworks, you can increase the odds of getting what you desire not by pounding home a hard sell, but by cuing into others' needs and addressing them.

ROCKING THE Q&A[1]

Key Insight

It's one thing to shine while giving a formal presentation. But how can we handle those less structured question and answer sessions that follow? And how can we handle impromptu questioning in meetings and one-on-one situations such as interviews? Many speakers dread these sessions, perceiving them as a gauntlet they must run and fearing that any mistake they make might undermine their credibility. If we reframe Q&A as a *dialogue* with audience members rather than dodgeball, we can unlock new opportunities to engage others and expand and extend our content. We can command the room and stay in control.

Why It Matters

I might sound overly optimistic in describing Q&A as an opportunity, but these sessions do afford you a number of advantages that formal portions of your presentation or meetings do not. First, you have the chance to project a sense of authenticity and veracity with your audience. They know you're not reading from a script here—your true personality is coming out, quirks and all. By allowing your (relatively) unvarnished self to come through, you can establish a deeper rapport with audience members, coming across as approachable and warm. Because you're interacting with audience members or meeting participants as individuals, you also can gain more insight into *their* personal beliefs and qualities.

Q&A sessions allow you to clarify your thinking and expand on points you might not have had time to address in your prior communication. As you demonstrate an ability to answer questions on the fly, you convey your mastery of the subject matter, enhancing your credibility rather than diminishing it.

The end result: more audience engagement, a sharper focus on your content, and a humanizing or personalizing of your messages.

Craft Your Content

When answering questions in the moment, you can add value for audience members by following a simple method that I call ADD:

A   **Answer the question:** First, answer the question in a single, clear, declarative sentence.

D   **Detail an example:** Second, provide specific, concrete evidence that supports your answer.

D   **Describe the value:** Finally, provide the benefits that explain why your answer is relevant and salient to the asker.

You need not perform these steps in order. A good response to a question simply provides an answer, concrete detail, and a statement about relevance or value. The concrete detail is critical. As listeners, we tend to remember details more than generalities. By providing color commentary, we help our audience to remember our response. By taking care to establish relevance, we make our message more urgent, engaging them even more.

I've found ADD so helpful that I've taught it to prospective job candidates while serving as a hiring manager. At the beginning of interviews, I told candidates that I would be asking them a series of questions and would like them to provide an answer, back it up with some detail, and then explain the relevance of this answer (how it would help them in the job were they to get it). The results were amazing. Candidates offered up answers that were much clearer, and they seemed to feel less anxious knowing that they had a format to follow. I was able to determine better who would make a good addition to my team.

Let's consider the steps of ADD in turn.

THINK FASTER, TALK SMARTER

Step #1: Answer the Question

As clearly and concisely as possible, provide a direct answer to the question that is asked of you. No need to provide a preamble or detailed background. Get to your answer directly. Delay tactics or straying from the point might undercut your response's transparency and authenticity, thus diminishing your credibility.

Examples:

If you made a formal presentation as part of a job interview and an audience member follows up by asking about your experience, you might say, "I have over fifteen years of experience in this field."

If you're presenting a progress report for your team at a big company meeting and an executive in the audience asks why your project is behind schedule, you might respond, "Supply chain issues and logistics delays have slowed us down."

Step #2: Detail a Concrete Example

Think of a key example that supports your answer. Don't go overboard on the specifics. Although some elaboration helps, too much risks boring audience members, distracting them, and turning them off. Keep this portion of your answer to a few sentences, offering a handful of details.

Examples:

"I have worked for three companies [name them], defining the scope of new projects, facilitating cross-functional teams, and presenting results to executives."

"For example, the materials we use to build the product foundation were delayed at the port for ten additional days due to tariff issues."

Step #3: Describe the Benefits and Relevance to the Asker

We often assume that people can immediately understand why our answer is important and relevant. Unfortunately, that's not always true.

To help our audience understand the value of our response and increase perceptions of our competence, we must be explicit about the most important benefits they stand to realize:

Examples:

"This means I can more quickly identify challenges and provide potential solutions to the issues you and your team are confronting."

"We have initiated contracts with additional suppliers and have looked into alternate transport methods to reduce future delays."

Unlike the first example, this second one addresses a negative issue. In such situations, we can use the "detail relevance" step to share what we are doing to remedy the issue at hand. Let's imagine that we're applying for a job, and someone raises a negative issue, asking us to identify a personal area in which we need to improve. We might answer with the following:

"I can get caught up in responding to emails and Slack messages and become distracted from my workflow [Answer]. For example, I often have twenty messages in my inbox at the beginning of every shift, and this slows me down from starting my tasks [Detail]. I now set a ten-minute reminder on my phone. When I hear the alarm go off, I know that I should stop responding to messages and start my other work tasks [Benefits/ Relevance]."

Refine Your Remarks

The ADD framework helps us avoid long-winded answers when confronted with questions. We dive in quickly and assertively, giving our audiences only what they need for our answer to seem meaningful and memorable. To enhance the power of ADD and add even more value via your responses, try the following:

Tip #1: Prepare for Possible Questions in Advance

Although Q&A sessions are spontaneous, we need not go in entirely cold. Think through potential questions in advance. What topics did you spend the most time preparing for in your initial presentation? What are some of the toughest queries you can imagine? Are there ones that you just *know* someone will ask you? Is there anything that you know about the audience ahead of time that might help you think about what types of queries they may have?

Once you've identified likely questions, map out via ADD how you might answer them most convincingly. Then go further and think of these questions as opportunities to expand on your material. Which favorite themes or points of yours might you address in the course of answering these queries? Think, too, about whether you might adjust your formal presentation or meeting agenda in ways that preempt these questions or put you in a better position to answer them.

If you struggle to think of compelling answers while doing this prep work, think of how you might quickly find answers—perhaps by reaching out to a knowledgeable contact of yours or doing a few minutes of online research. As you come up with satisfactory answers, try speaking them out loud. You might record yourself answering and then playing it back to see how you sound. If you can't find answers, think through how you might respond in the moment. When I don't know an answer to a question posed in Q&A, I always acknowledge that I don't know and promise audiences that I'll get back to them within a set period of time.

Tip #2: Time the Q&A to Your Advantage

Q&A often happens at the end of presentations and meetings, but not always. If your presentation covers multiple topics or is organized into at least two parts, it might make sense to pause and take questions as a way of transitioning from one part to the next. In general, you shouldn't speak for more than ten minutes without checking in with your audience through questioning. This will engage them and allow you a chance to see if they're following along. On the other hand, pausing too often might make your overall presentation or meeting too long. It can also interrupt the flow and make it hard to stay focused. If your presentation is shorter than five minutes, handling questions at the end might be a better idea.

If you are new to a topic or feel nervous, I would suggest waiting until the end of your presentation to take questions. Your confidence might build as you go along, and you might find yourself picking up cues from audience members about the points of yours that seem to be landing especially well. This knowledge could inform how you answer questions later on. It will also allow you to get through the material that you have prepared for the most. That way, if an unexpected question comes up at the end, you won't find yourself becoming derailed from your content's flow.

Whenever you opt to take questions, set expectations at the outset with your audience. If they know in advance that you'll be taking questions at the end, you reduce the likelihood that they'll be raising their hands to interrupt in the middle. They might also decide to write down their questions so that they remember to ask them later. Clearly outlining the structure of your presentation, including where you will pause for questions, sets expectations about the pace of what's to come and puts everyone at ease.

Tip #3: Maintain Control by Setting Boundaries

When handling Q&A, you have more control than you might realize. In setting expectations for your audience, you can define how many questions you'll field, how much time you have for this spontaneous dialogue, and what kinds of topics are fair game for questions. Be sure to set these boundaries clearly, as doing so allows you to decline to answer questions if they violate your preset parameters.

You might say, "At the end of my talk, I'll have about ten minutes to answer any questions you might have about the new project my team has been working on and the market potential it has." Or if you're in a job interview, you might say, "I'm happy to answer questions that pertain to my previous jobs."

When it comes time to field questions, keep a firm hand on the proceedings. Many speakers open the Q&A portion of their presentations by saying, "Are there any questions?" *Bad idea.* Some audience members might take that as a license to ask far-ranging questions that have little to do with the subject of your presentation. If you set expectations at the outset, remind audience members of them. "Now, does anyone have any questions about our new project? Again, I'll have about ten minutes."

Tip #4: End Q&A Sessions with an Exclamation Point

Let's say you've applied the ADD formula and these other tips and as a result are really rocking the Q&A. The last thing you want to do is flop when ending the session. Many speakers end awkwardly, muttering "thanks" or "okay, I guess we're done here" before sauntering off the stage. You do want to thank your audience for their attention, but add some extra oomph to your exit by reminding audience members once more of your key message or ideas. You might say, "Thank you for your questions. Clearly, we must invest in this project to achieve our goals," or "I really appreciate your questions and input. Together we can launch this initiative successfully." Think about the single idea you want listeners to glean from your presentation or meeting and end with that. If you reflect on potential closing lines in advance, you know you'll be able to end on a high note no matter what.

Tip #5: Play the Conductor When Answering with Others

At panel discussions, team meetings, and other situations, it often isn't just a single individual who is presenting to an audience, but several speakers working together as a team. When it is time for Q&A with multiple presenters, the discussion can break down due to lack of coordination: either nobody jumps in to answer a query, or multiple people do, vying for the floor.

You can manage this situation more smoothly by adopting the "orchestra conductor" approach. Before the session, assign one of the speakers to play the role of conductor during the Q&A. As questions arise, this person will field them and then farm them out to themselves or other speakers depending on what they know about the various speakers' expertise, seniority within the group, or interest level. A good conductor will ensure that all speakers get appropriate airtime. With a conductor directing queries, in some cases literally pointing or gesturing as a musical conductor does, the entire session comes across as more organized, fluid, and controlled.

Tip #6: Ask Yourself a Question If None Come In

As Q&A sessions kick off, it's not always easy to get audience members to pose that first question. This is understandable. Like you, your audience is transitioning from what had been a monologue to a dialogue. Audience members might feel shy or embarrassed to speak, especially if the audience is a large one. They might want to pose a question but feel reluctant to go first.

If you invite the audience to ask questions and nobody raises their hand or steps up to the microphone right away, take a pause and wait. Jittery speakers won't do that—they'll rush to observe that nobody has any questions and close down the proceedings. That feels weak to me. Surely *someone* must have a question.

In some cases, that someone might have to be you. If you've paused for several seconds (I advise waiting for a full five) and nobody has raised their hands, pose what I call a "back-pocket" question. Have a question ready in your figurative back pocket for precisely this situation. Make it a question you want to answer and one you can easily handle. You might preface it by saying, "A question people often ask me is . . ." or "When I first began learning about this topic, one thing that puzzled me was . . ."

Often, simply posing and answering that first question is enough to break the ice, increasing the odds that someone else will pose a second question. If audience members still don't come forward with queries, then you can feel free to wrap up the proceedings at this point. In this case, it will not have been a Q&A session for the ages, but at least a question has been posed—and answered.

Application in Action

As I've suggested, we might find ourselves fielding questions in a wide range of scenarios—when we're serving as panelists at a professional conference, being interviewed on a podcast, meeting with our boss to explain our past performance, or even getting to know a potential special someone on a first date. The following scenarios evoke these situations, suggesting how you might apply ADD to answer succinctly and powerfully. Notice how the inclusion of detail and the attention paid to relevance make for more satisfying answers in the moment.

Scenario #1

You're in a job interview, and the hiring manager across the table asks you to describe a recent challenge that you had to overcome.

A possible response:

First, set a boundary by pointing out that you will focus on challenges from your most recent job, not other areas of your professional life. Then go on to give your answer. Your answer might look something like this: "About six months ago, I worked with a colleague who failed to deliver his work in a timely manner, which often jeopardized our group's ability to complete our task [A]. He failed to submit his user report that served as the foundation for our corrective action plan [D]. To address this problem, I pulled him aside and offered to help with his deliverables. I asked that he let us know two days in advance if he needed assistance. I always try to be direct with challenging situations and offer to assist [D]." Remember that when answering questions about challenges or areas of improvement you can use the relevance part of your answer (the second D) to explain your correction or plan so that your interviewer gets insight into how you will act in the future.

Scenario #2

You're participating in a podcast or fireside chat interview. The interviewer asks you to share a bit about your connection to the topic under discussion.

A possible response:

The key here is to really connect to the audience who is listening in. What value will they take from your participation in the event? Your answer could be something like "I am passionate about communication [A]. I have studied, taught, and coached communication skills for over twenty-five years in a variety of settings [D]. I am really excited to share some of what I have learned over my many years to help you and your audience to feel more comfortable and confident in their communication [D]."

Scenario #3

You're at a mixer and you're getting to know someone new. You ask one another generic questions to break the ice. The other person asks you what brings you there that day.

A possible response:

"Well, I always enjoy learning new things and meeting people [A]. I found the goal of this gathering to be really interesting and educational [D]. I hope to share some of my past experiences and look forward to learning from folks like you [D]."

Scenario #4

You're in a meeting with your boss, and they're grilling you about your team's focus and productivity.

A possible response:

"For the past two weeks, we have been focused on customer service concerns [A]. We have received twenty percent more calls about two specific features in our product since we released the new upgrade [D]. We have recently created some online tutorials that we are now providing customers when they initially call. This is allowing my team members to refocus on their other tasks. Further, we plan to create new online tutorials and send them out proactively prior to our next upgrade [D]."

Notice how in this answer, referring to specific data or numbers can really help. This is another way in which using details can reinforce and strengthen our answer.

Parting Thought

Some time ago, a former student of mine founded a small consulting company that helped firms transition from storing data on their physical premises to the cloud. Over time, my student realized that he could grow his business faster if they automated the transition process by selling tools that would do the work for customers rather than human consultants. Under his leadership, the company embarked on a shift from selling consulting services to selling software.

As you can imagine, the consultants and other employees who worked for my student were alarmed. Some feared losing their jobs, while others wondered if they'd do as well selling the company's software products after selling its consulting services for so long. To keep the company together, my student would need to communicate the company's strategic choices to his employees, opening himself at times to some very frank and pointed questioning.

We worked together to help him build his skills in spontaneous Q&A situations. I taught him the ADD formula, and we practiced how he'd handle certain kinds of questions. He found the ADD structure quite helpful. The clarity of his positions buttressed his credibility, as did his mastery of detail. It made a huge difference that he took care to explain how his answers were relevant to employees, customers, and the company's mission and vision. Even if employees didn't like everything he said, they perceived that he was speaking to *them* and their concerns. They felt they were getting straight talk from their boss, and that his answers were focused and well considered.

My student's answers didn't take up airtime. They added value. As a result, he didn't just survive difficult questioning during this emotionally charged chapter in his company's history. Rather, he turned spontaneous queries into an opportunity to build stronger connections with his people, get the right messages across, and enhance his stature as a leader.

Don't let spontaneous queries scare you. Let ADD's three simple steps empower you to take control and engage in a dialogue with others. Instead of reacting defensively, you can reinforce your ideas and convey them in more meaningful ways. Instead of diminishing your credibility, you can ADD value.

FEEDBACK THAT DOESN'T FLOP

Key Insight

When providing feedback, we often stand in judgment of others, seeking to impart wisdom or tell others what to do. If we instead frame feedback as an invitation to solve problems collaboratively, we'll often find that we achieve better short-term results while bolstering our relationship with others over the long term.

Why It Matters

When we focus on telling others what we think, we risk establishing or perpetuating a power dynamic that prevents others from really hearing us. By positioning ourselves as authoritative judges of others, we speak from on high, putting the recipients of feedback in the position of passively listening. In a best-case scenario, we convey the information we want but miss a chance to work collaboratively. Worse, we risk putting the feedback recipient on the defensive, coming across as rigid, punishing, or demanding.

When we regard feedback as an invitation to solve a problem together, we shift the dynamics of the conversation. Instead of inducing a defensive reaction, we can establish a shared sense of ownership, openness, and accountability. We're no longer directing others, telling them what to do. Rather, we're huddling with them on the same level, working as a team to improve what we're doing or how we're behaving. Proceeding on this basis, we stand a far better chance of spurring real progress and strengthening—not weakening—our relationships.

Craft Your Content

A useful structure for providing feedback in the moment that is both inviting and collaborative is something I call the 4 I's:

- **Information:** First, provide concrete, specific observations of the action or approach about which you will be providing feedback.
- **Impact:** Second, explain the effect the action or approach has on you.
- **Invitation:** Third, extend a collaboration request to address the action or approach on which you are providing feedback.
- **Implications:** Fourth, detail the positive and/or negative consequences for adopting or not adopting the changes you are suggesting.

Cover each of these I's in turn and you can present a clear, constructive message that hopefully will invite a positive future outcome.

Step #1: Provide Information

Begin your remarks by presenting objective observations about the other person or their work. As difficult as it might be, leave out any emotion on your part—stick to facts that are readily evident and verifiable.

Examples:
If you're a boss giving feedback to a direct report who was late in submitting a recent report, you might say, "As you may have seen, your report on our customers' NPS scores was late and didn't make it into our board deck for the upcoming board meeting."

If you're a teacher giving feedback to a student, you might say, "You earned an A on your first exam but C-minuses on your last two."

Be sure to delineate what you're *not* going to discuss. In the first example, you might say, "I'd like to talk to you today about the timeliness of your report, not its quality." In the second, "Your in-class participation is great, but I'd like us to discuss the effort you're putting in on your exams." By scoping the conversation this way, you help both the recipient and yourself to focus.

Step #2: Explain the Impact

With salient facts on the table, explain your thoughts and feelings about the change you wish to see in the other person's work or behavior. Speak directly using the first-person singular (for example, "I think" or "I feel"). You want to own your thoughts and feelings, since that will allow you to demonstrate the issue's importance to you. Taking full responsibility for your reaction also will help to reduce the defensiveness and sense of being blamed that the other person may feel.

Examples:
"I know the board is unclear on the customer satisfaction progress that we've made in the last quarter, and I fear we may have missed an opportunity to show board members how our initiatives paid off."

"I worry that you're not meeting the goals we established this semester, and I'm concerned that you might not get a final grade for the course that will set you up for admission to your favorite colleges."

When framing the problem that you must discuss and solve, be explicit about why it matters. Direct reports might not understand how their work fits into a bigger picture, and all team members will benefit from a clear message about the importance of what they're doing. A student might not have the experience or background to understand how their failure to take their studies seriously might impact their future success.

Step #3: Extend an Invitation

Make a request of the other person, one that is specific and concise and that if honored will lead to the change or improvement you seek. You can frame this request as a question to encourage deeper participation or as a declarative sentence that better evokes the direction of your collaboration.

Examples:

"How can we ensure that your report gets submitted to the CEO's chief of staff before the deadline?" or "I encourage you to get your report to the CEO's chief of staff twenty-four hours before the board meeting presentation deck deadline."

"How might we work together to ensure that you're better prepared for the next exam?" or "I need you to attend my Friday tutoring session prior to the next exam."

Word choice matters in all communication, and especially when providing feedback. Using "we" and posing a question puts both of you on the same level, establishing the desired change as the result of a joint effort. It affords the recipient of feedback a bit of agency or autonomy in resolving the situation. You're implying that their perspective matters, too—it's a part of the solution to be welcomed, not a part of the problem to be shunted aside.

Likewise, framing the invitation declaratively instead of posing a question can help clarify or accentuate your invitation. This directness might be especially appropriate if you have provided feedback on this issue before or are pressed for time.

Step #4: Detail the Implications
Finally, lay out what will happen if the other person chooses either to comply or reject the feedback. You can provide positive, negative, or combined consequences.

Examples:

"By ensuring the NPS scores are in the board deck, we'll demonstrate our commitment to our customers and highlight the important work your team does." Or "If the board doesn't see the NPS scores in their deck, they're likely to question our commitment to our customer satisfaction OKR, and

they might choose to restructure our customer services organization."

"Getting an A on your next exam will mean that you'll receive
an A-minus for your final grade. Think of how good you will
feel finishing the quarter that way." Or "If we don't find a way
for you to improve your test scores, you might find it hard to
make the grades required to play your sport."

Refine Your Remarks

Keeping the 4 I's handy when we deliver feedback on the fly can make
our comments crisper, cleaner, and more collaborative. But how precisely
we execute on the 4 I's matters, too. Here are some tips to keep in mind:

Tip #1: Prepare
If we're entering a situation where we think we might have to deliver
feedback, we can hone our message by asking questions of ourselves
beforehand:

- Why might the person behave in ways we don't like?
- What do we gain or lose by giving feedback—or by refrain-
  ing from giving it?
- What behavior would we *like* to see?

When we begin a conversation in which we're delivering feedback,
we might inquire what level or type of feedback the person would benefit from or want. Doing so not only allows us to focus our remarks; it
shows that we hope to engage collaboratively. We might also ask ourselves whether our feedback is likely to help. If not, we might decide at
the last moment not to offer it. For example, when a colleague shares
his frustration about a meeting we both attended, I can check in first
and ask if he is looking for support and advice or a catharsis. Understanding his needs in the moment, help me to determine how best to
respond.

When my wife asks me for feedback on something she has done, she often winds up giving *me* "constructive" ideas for how I might better deliver my feedback. I tend to offer suggestions and provide alternatives when sharing my impressions. She would prefer that I focus on how she is feeling. As a result, I now make a practice of asking her what type of feedback she most desires before sharing my opinions.

Tip #2: Be Timely

We can achieve much better results with feedback that is timely, whether given spontaneously or not. When a person has done something that calls for feedback, we should speak up as soon after the offending behavior has occurred as possible. Of course, we also must allow time for strong emotions we might feel to settle. Choose the first occasion in which you can deliver feedback calmly and effectively. If for some reason you can't give feedback right after the offending event has occurred, try at least to alert the person(s) involved that you would like to chat very soon about what transpired. Putting a "pin" on this event will alert them to remember this moment.

Tip #3: Respect the Context

An important caveat about timely feedback is to remember that the setting for providing the feedback also matters. Are we in the right place to deliver feedback and achieve our desired impact? Is it a good time given what else the recipient is experiencing or dealing with at the moment?

People often best receive feedback when everyone involved is prepared and in the right mental and physical place to hear it. We might encounter a friend or colleague in a crowded public venue and feel tempted to deliver feedback. If the subject at hand is serious, that might not be such a good idea. Perhaps they're distracted with other tasks. Perhaps they would feel more comfortable speaking privately. Perhaps they're having a bad day and can't engage with you calmly and thoughtfully—you've arrived at a "nonteachable moment," as veteran volleyball coach Ruben Nieves calls it.[1] Perhaps the feedback's unexpected arrival makes it difficult for them to receive it.

When we think about context, we also should aim to deliver feedback in person if possible rather than in virtual settings. It can be more challenging to deliver feedback effectively online, in writing, or on the phone, since we can't always cue in to how others are receiving what we're saying, nor can we do much to tailor the setting to the message we wish to deliver.[2]

Tip #4: Adopt the Right Tone

The precise tone we use can dramatically change the meaning of feedback we give using the 4 I's. Let's say a colleague has arrived ten minutes late for a meeting for the third time. Applying the 4 I's, we might say: "Hey, I noticed you're ten minutes late. This is the third time that's happened. I feel you're not prioritizing this meeting in the same way that I am. Are there ways that we can work together to help you be here on time so that we won't be late in completing our project?"

To add urgency, we might adopt a sterner tone in applying the 4 I's, something like "You were ten minutes late to our meeting. I feel you're not prioritizing this meeting appropriately. I need you to arrive ten minutes early to the next meeting. If you don't, we might have to remove you from the team."

Notice the differences. The first rendition takes a collaborative tone because we're asking a question and offering to participate in the solution. In the second rendition, our feedback is a sharp declaration that also comes across as harsher because we point to negative implications arising from a failure to comply. Knowing that tone matters and that we can influence our tone in the moment can help us to convey our message more clearly.

Tip #5: Stay Balanced

In every spontaneous encounter, we shouldn't strive merely to offer critical feedback but positive feedback as well. Before launching into the 4 I's, you may benefit from saying something positive about the recipient. Leading with a positive comment not only reinforces that you find value in the recipient and their efforts; it also will likely increase their receptivity to your constructive feedback. Of course, others should perceive your praise as roughly similar in importance as your constructive feedback. Praising someone on their outfit and then informing them that the quality of their work is deficient might come across as awkward, forced, or disingenuous. You would do better instead to praise them for real contributions they've made, such as raising important questions in a recent meeting or continuing to support the company's new hires.

Tip #6: Monitor Emotions

As we provide feedback, we should pay close attention to the way the recipient is responding. If they become defensive, emotional, or distracted, we must adjust our message. Likewise, we can attend to our own emotional state during the conversation. Are we becoming too heated to communicate effectively? Might we dial up or down the emotional content of what we're saying to convey our ideas more effectively? If the situation starts to become emotionally charged, consider acknowledging the emotions without naming them and then returning to more objective matters. It can be risky to name emotions. If I observe that you seem upset, you might reply, "No, I'm not—I'm frustrated." We end up debating the emotional state instead of focusing on solving the problem at hand. To acknowledge emotions without naming them, you might say something like "I can hear in your voice how important this is to you. I know we can find a good solution by focusing on a clear schedule."

Tip #7: Stay Focused

We might have multiple pieces of feedback to deliver in the moment, not just one. A good rule of thumb: less is more. Beware of drowning the recipient in too much feedback, as they might have trouble absorbing any of it. What are the one or two changes we'd most like to see the other person make or the one or two most important things you want them to know? Focus on those and leave additional feedback for another time.

Application in Action

The following three scenarios evoke the variety of different spontaneous feedback situations you might find yourself in, including situations in which others ask for feedback from you and those in which you find it necessary to give feedback to others because of behavior you're witnessing. I've also tried to suggest how you might respond in situations where you possess more or less power or status than the other person. In all of these situations, you have several levers at your disposal, including word choice, how you frame invitations (as questions, suggestions, or declarations), and where or in front of whom you deliver the feedback. The more comfortable you become with the 4 I's, the more you'll be able to focus on these levers to communicate with appropriate nuance.

Scenario #1
Your colleague calls you over and asks you to review an email they plan to send to a prospective client. The email as written is vague and confusing.

A possible response:
"I notice that your email is three paragraphs long and does not end with a clear request [Information]. I would be confused if I received this message [Impact]. I have two suggestions: (1) remove the summary of your last meeting and simply put a link to the meeting notes and (2) put your desired action in the email subject line [Invitation]. By making these changes, I think the prospect will be more likely to respond quickly [Implication]."

Scenario #2
Whenever your boss presents to your team, he tends to focus on and favor the input of men on your team over women. This makes many of the women feel uncomfortable, impacting their morale.

A possible response:
"I just wanted to bring to your attention that when you asked for input today, you only called on men and did not allow women raising their hands to speak [Information]. I fear this is sending a message to the women on my team that you don't value their work as much as that of the men [Impact]. Are there things I can do to help you involve the women on my team more [Invitation]? If we can address this issue, I think you'll find that

all of my team members have useful insights that will help us solve the specific challenges you bring to us [Implication]."

Scenario #3

You and your child are attending a social event. Other guests are mingling and getting to know one another, yet your child is engrossed in their phone and not engaged.

A possible response:

"You were looking down at your phone and didn't respond to the last two people who greeted you [Information]. I feel it's impolite for you not to be involved with the people around you [Impact]. Please silence your phone and put it away for the next ten to fifteen minutes [Invitation]. If you do continue to be on your phone, I will have to take it away from you until we get home [Implication]."

Parting Thought

In recent years, I've helped to advise a Stanford PhD student who went on to teach communications at an Ivy League school. "Alice" and I developed a great relationship, collaborating in a number of ways. Soon after she began teaching, Alice called to say that she was very upset: she received her first batch of student evaluations, and they were poor. Although students appreciated the value of what she was teaching, they felt that she was throwing too much dense material at them. Alice wanted my feedback: Should she take her students' criticisms to heart? And what did I think about how she was reacting to their negative evaluations?

Applying the 4 I's structure in the moment, I pointed out that on her syllabus she had many assignments and readings due at once, and that many of her due dates fell on Mondays, which meant her students likely needed to work a lot on the weekends (Information). I further observed that with some simple adjustments, she could tweak her syllabus to conform better to her students' schedules. I shared with her that she need not feel threatened by negative responses from students

(Impact). Encouraging her to problem-solve, I provided my syllabus as an example of how she might better time the due dates of her assignments (Invitation). Finally, I suggested that if she acted upon her students' feedback, she would likely be able to improve her teaching, leading to better evaluations later on (Implications).

Alice took my feedback to heart, shifting how she thought about her students' responses and how she designed her class assignments and readings. A semester later, she called to say that she had received another round of student evaluations and was elated: the response this time to her teaching was much more positive. She thanked me for the feedback and support that I gave her. As a result of this episode, our relationship strengthened, and new opportunities for professional collaboration opened up.

Giving feedback is one way that we can demonstrate concern and care for others. Taking time to do it so that it lands well can help others in the moment, and it also can foster longer-term connection, respect, and credibility. Inviting collaboration makes all the difference.

THE SECRETS
TO SAYING WE'RE SORRY

Key Insight

Many of the skills we've covered in this book have helped you to put your best foot forward when speaking spontaneously. But what happens when you make a mistake? How can you best address and manage a situation when you have somehow caused offense or behaved improperly?

Knowing how to apologize well is a useful skill to have, especially when we try to take more risks in spontaneous situations and let our true selves shine. But so many of us don't know the secrets to saying we're sorry. If we've caused offense to others, we worsen the situation by apologizing poorly, inappropriately, or not at all. Others come away feeling frustrated and perceive us as tone-deaf, insincere, or disrespectful. Rather than effectively communicating with an audience in a way that forms connection and collaboration, failing to address missteps when they inevitably occur can lead to conflict and resentment. We can avoid this outcome by understanding the key components of a meaningful apology and weaving them together into a single, coherent framework.

Why It Matters

"Never apologize, mister, it's a sign of weakness."[1] Thus opined a character played by John Wayne in the 1949 film *She Wore a Yellow Ribbon*.

It's a classic misconception, one adopted by some public figures today who either refrain from offering apologies or do so only reluctantly. To be clear: Apologizing is not a sign of weakness. It's an act of courage and strength. It shows that we care about our relationships—even those we have with acquaintances and strangers—and are willing to set aside our own ego for the sake of creating a comfortable and constructive environment for everyone.

Apologies can serve a variety of purposes in the context of relationships. Most obviously, they can reduce the anger and frustration that others feel toward us and reduce the chances that they'll try to get even. They can reassure others that we won't repeat our offending behavior, in the process inviting trust and future interactions. A well-crafted apology can help others see that we're not really jerks, and that our bad behavior was situational—we meant well but on this occasion weren't able to behave at our best. Apologies can also help us to project empathy and deepen our connection with the person we've offended.

Craft Your Content

To ensure that your apology hits the mark, structure it using a formula that I call AAA. Think of it as emergency roadside assistance—it's useful to have when you're in a bind. The formula is as follows:

A **Acknowledge:** First, Identify the offending behavior and take responsibility for it.

A **Appreciate:** Second, publicly accept how your offense has impacted others.

A **Amends:** Third, detail how you will make up for your offense, specifying what action you will take or refrain from taking to remedy the situation or how your thinking will change.

There is no one-size-fits-all apology that works for all situations. Individuals whom we've wronged will evaluate our apology in light of how serious our misdeeds and their impacts are. Although a well-structured apology might suffice if we happen to have come five minutes late to a meeting, it might not if we've inadvertently insulted or embarrassed

THINK FASTER, TALK SMARTER

someone. Regardless of the seriousness of our transgressions, those whom we've hurt want to see us own up to what we've done; acknowledge the impact it has had on them, particularly on an emotional level; and understand how we intend to make amends. By combining these three elements into a structure, we can ensure that every apology we offer stands the best chance of smoothing over hurt feelings and projecting our empathy. Let's take a closer look at these elements and how to execute them.

Step #1: Acknowledge the Action and Accept Responsibility
We often hear people utter non-apologies that never acknowledge the action or take clear responsibility. They might say, "I'm sorry if what I said offended you," as if everything we said was fine and reasonable people probably wouldn't take offense at our remarks. They might say, "I sometimes don't think before speaking," failing to directly specify that they are apologizing for a specific remark that caused offense. They might say, "I'm sorry for offending you, but I was upset because of what you said about me," offering an explanation that seems to blame others or the situation at hand and excuse themselves of all or some of the responsibility.

Don't try to justify, minimize, or explain away your behavior when issuing an apology. Don't apologize for how you made someone feel. You need to own what you actually did or did not do for an apology to land. Clearly describe the action that you took or failed to take. Be specific—don't hide behind generalities. Remember, apologizing takes courage. Don't wiggle out by offering a subtle or slippery non-apology.

Examples:
"I'm sorry that I waited until the last minute to test the system out."

"I apologize for using only male pronouns and names in my examples."

"I'm sorry I questioned your commitment to our project in front of others."

Step #2: Appreciate the Impact

Once you've specified an action that you regret, you can now project empathy for others. You should make it clear that your action wasn't only wrong but also damaging in some way. You should show others that you understand the full impact and consequences of your action or inaction, including the emotional consequences it had for the people you've wronged.

You might feel tempted to minimize your impact, but this would be a big mistake. The person harmed by your action or inaction bears the emotional brunt of what you've done. Any attempt to "put it into perspective" not only devalues their reaction but also serves to reduce your burden. In apologizing to your teenage child, you might tell them that it was "no big deal" when you pecked them on the cheek in front of their friends while dropping them off at school, but you must remember that this little kiss might well be a big deal to them, causing them to lose social status and feel embarrassed. You come across as defensive and insensitive, perhaps making the situation even worse. In any situation when you're extending an apology, you should show as best you can that you really do "get" why your behavior was so problematic and hurtful.

Examples:

"Having to wait for a lengthy software upgrade to install cut into valuable work time that you needed for your project."

"Using masculine terminology diminishes the value of women's contributions to this work and is demotivating."

"By questioning your commitment publicly, I made you look bad in front of the team and implied that your contribution was less valuable than those of others on the team."

Step #3: Detail How You Will Make Amends

If you take responsibility for a misdeed and acknowledge its effects but don't signal your willingness to make amends, your apology won't carry much weight. Poorly led companies make this mistake all the time. They project empathy and take responsibility when their products fail and cause harm, but then they offer only vague statements about their intention to "do better." They don't lay out clear steps that they plan to take. Somehow, nothing ever seems to change. This in turn causes customers to lose faith in these companies and become cynical.

Avoid damaging your relationships by specifying what you'll do in the immediate future to reduce the chances that your offense will happen again. By being specific, you show the person you've wronged that you're serious about making amends, and you implicitly invite them to hold you accountable.

Examples:
"To avoid this happening again, I will test the system one hour before we do our demonstrations. And I will do this starting next week."

"Before our next meeting, I will be sure to find a more diverse set of examples to use so that I don't rely just on male stories and names."

"The next time I have any issues with your performance, I'll speak to you in private about it."

Refine Your Remarks[2]

Using AAA to frame your apologies allows you and the person you've wronged to process what happened effectively and productively. Yet, it's not enough to simply get the structure right. How and when we deliver it matters as well. Here are some further thoughts on how you might enhance your use of AAA and improve the impact of your apologies.

Tip #1: Don't Pre-apologize
If you're entering a situation in which you think you might make a misstep, it can be tempting to try to cut your losses by asking for forgiveness

first. You might say "I might wind up being thirty minutes late, so let me apologize in advance." Or perhaps "I'm going to be very busy networking during the cocktail party, so please excuse me if I ignore you." Or "I have a lot of material here, so our Zoom might run long." Or "I am really nervous; I apologize in advance if I stumble over my words."

Although you might intend such pre-apologies to show your regard for the other person's feelings, these statements usually backfire. They typically leave the other person wondering about your sincerity: If you know that your timing isn't aligned with the scheduled meeting time, why did you not adjust for that ahead of time or edit your presentation to fit the time allotted? If you really cared about their feelings, wouldn't you modify your behavior? A pre-apology also serves to draw your audience's attention to your offense, leading them to look for it and remember it more when it happens.

If you suspect you might offend someone, clarify your priorities in your own mind. If you can change your plans or behavior without inconveniencing yourself unduly so that you don't cause offense, do it. If you can't, do your best and apologize after the fact.

Tip #2: Don't Wait Too Long to Apologize

It's true that it's better to apologize late than not at all, and situational factors can prevent you from apologizing right away. If you disrespected a colleague by speaking over them at a meeting with the CEO, it might be safest to wait until after the meeting to say something rather than in the moment. If you said something insulting to your child while seeing them off to school, you might have to wait until they get home that evening to make it right.

In general, though, as I suggested when discussing feedback, the sooner we can apologize after our offending act, the better. That way, we can prevent resentment and anger from festering. If we apologize so quickly that others actually see us catching ourselves in the act of making a mistake and then taking responsibility, we might leave them with a clearer sense of our good intentions. A timely apology also relieves us of the stress that can come from that nagging sense that we've wronged someone. By saying something promptly, we can both move on.

Tip #3: Be Specific, Clear, and Brief

When it comes to apologies, just enough is usually plenty. When we feel guilty about something we've done, the anxiety over how it made us look or made other people feel can sometimes become overpowering. We may be mortified about what happened and feel anxious about the damage we've done, so we keep apologizing profusely in hopes of driving home our point. Repeating an apology might make us feel better in the moment, but the person we've wronged might find it annoying or even potentially harassing. By overemphasizing what we've done, we risk inflating it in the other person's mind, causing them to become more offended than they otherwise might have been. If we're accurately assessing the damage we've done, over-apologizing may not give the other person a chance to cool down, making the situation worse.

As hard as it might be, we should deliver a single, well-structured, sincere apology, and leave it at that. We should trust that the other person will also be gracious and reasonable enough to accept our contrition—if not in the moment, then later once they've had a chance to process and get a little distance.

We can over-apologize by repeating the same apology repetitively, and we can also do so by feeling compelled to apologize for our tiniest missteps. Every perceived transgression on our part however minute doesn't merit an apology. Should we roll out the AAA framework every time we're just a minute or two late for a meeting? Should we do so when we said something that is true, perfectly reasonable, and well-intentioned but that we fear might not have landed precisely right? If we offer apologies all the time, they mean less. Take a balanced and thoughtful approach to apologizing. When you feel pretty certain that you've overstepped in a meaningful way, offer a meaningful response. Treating others the way you would want to be treated is probably a pretty good rule to follow.

Application in Action

The AAA framework serves us in a wide range of situations and for transgressions big and small. For a sense of how we might best apply it, consider the following scenarios.

Scenario #1

Times are tough at work, and the stress has gotten to you. You lost your temper and reacted poorly in a meeting, showing disrespect to a colleague. Later that afternoon, you run into the colleague in a hallway and notice that they're upset.

A possible response:

"I'm very sorry that I raised my voice and cut you off when you were explaining your point of view. That was wrong of me [Acknowledge]. I know that my argumentativeness is unacceptable, and that it reduces how comfortable and collaborative people on our team feel [Appreciate]. Starting today, when I become really passionate, I'll wait my turn, speak more quietly, and summarize what I heard others say before I contribute my perspective [Action]."

The speaker here doesn't attempt to excuse their behavior. They simply delineate what they did that caused offense. In describing the impact, they reference not just how the offended party might have been affected, but also the negative consequences for the entire team. This increases the odds that the person who was offended will perceive that the speaker understands fully how damaging their behavior was. Further, it's important to avoid public shaming and private apologizing. In this situation, a public, timely apology would make a big difference.

Scenario #2

You're collaborating on a project with a colleague whose native language is different than yours. Because of the language gap, you stop asking this person for input, and they express frustration at being left out.

A possible response:

"I'm sorry. I was struggling to understand what you were saying and began to listen to and seek advice from others [Acknowledge]. I understand that this left you out of the conversation, which couldn't have felt good [Appreciate]. Let me ask everyone next time to contribute ideas in the chat window so that I can see everyone's contributions equally. That way, I will be able to concentrate more and better understand what you and everyone else is saying [Action]."

In this situation, the speaker's goal is a practical one: to ensure that everyone feels comfortable contributing even though it's sometimes hard to understand what people who are not native speakers are saying. Note that the second step conveys empathy, but in a subtle way. The speaker acknowledges that being left out of the conversation would have felt off-putting and perhaps even insulting.

Scenario #3
You're on a virtual call taking part in a high-pressure business meeting and are feeling nervous. You just realized to your distress that you mispronounced a person's name. You don't want to make a big deal of it, but you feel the need to apologize.

A possible response:
"I apologize for not saying your name correctly. How do you pronounce it [Acknowledge]? I can imagine that it feels uncomfortable to be called by the wrong name and that it might be challenging to correct me [Appreciate]. In the future, I will look over the list of participants and ask about pronunciations prior to starting the meeting [Action]."

In this situation, it's important that the speaker not only recognize publicly that they made the mistake, but that they also ask for the proper way to say the person's name. Doing so shows that the speaker is interested in fixing their mistake, and it also ensures that nobody else will repeat the mistake. Acknowledging the error as well as the potential discomfort in correcting it is key.

Parting Thought

Not long ago, I made a fairly significant faux pas while team-teaching a communication course with a colleague. We were discussing how important it is to provide context for the data we present, since audiences can find it numbing to encounter a stream of numbers without enough information to make sense or evaluate them. Not a subject that on its face would seem particularly offensive. Ah, but wait.

To make the point, I told the class a story about an executive I had coached some years earlier who was a senior leader at one of the world's largest banks. As part of his presentation, he referenced the astronomical amount of money that went through his bank every day. As I told the class, I advised my client not only to mention the amount of money but to give his audience some way to understand just how large this number was. The executive did some calculations and wound up mentioning in his presentation that the sum he was referencing amounted to 25 percent of the world's money.

In presenting this example, I initially felt quite satisfied with myself—my students would now remember better to make their own data come alive for their audiences. But then I noticed one of my students folding his arms in front of him and scowling at the wall. For the rest of the class, this normally passionate and talkative student stayed silent and pensive. Something I had said landed badly with my audience.

After class, I approached him to ask if everything was okay. He told me he had just had his house foreclosed on by the very bank I had used in my example. Hearing how much money went through the bank every day reminded him of a very difficult personal situation and made him feel worse about it.

I felt badly and offered up an apology using the AAA framework. I said that I was very sorry for mentioning the bank and their revenue. I told him that I understood how my example could have brought up negative emotions for him, and I promised to be as careful as I could in the future about avoiding examples that might feel painful or uncomfortable to my audience.

Without a structure to fall back on, I might have left out parts of the message that I wanted to convey or I might have rambled on and on. The AAA structure helped me to focus and provide a quick and concise apology, one that emphasized how my offense impacted my student. Appreciating my sensitivity and the timeliness of my response, my student quickly forgave me. During the next class, he was again engaged and enthusiastic. I, too, had learned a valuable lesson.

All of us make mistakes, which means that all of us stand to gain by learning the secrets of saying sorry. The AAA framework challenges us to behave empathetically and responsibly when we mess up, regardless of the emotions we might feel in the moment. It prompts us to step up, put our defensiveness and egos aside, and show a bit of humility and self-awareness as we mend a breach in our relationships. Contrary to popular belief, apologizing isn't weakness. Rather, it's one of the best ways available to us to show that we care and are striving to improve.

EPILOGUE

During the summer of 2022, a former student of mine, the Australian swimmer Annabelle Williams, found herself in a spontaneous communications situation that most people would find nightmarish and impossible to handle. A Paralympic gold medalist who set five world records, Williams was serving as a color commentator on live television for swimming events held as part of the Commonwealth Games. One day, she received an urgent phone call from her network: a colleague was unexpectedly out, and Williams's boss wanted her to fill in at the last minute as cohost of its prime-time broadcast.

This was a breakout opportunity for Williams. She had never cohosted a prime-time broadcast. This portion of the coverage had a large audience—more than a million viewers. She felt anxious. Commentators typically spend weeks doing research in preparation for hosting a major sporting event. That way, when action takes place or there is dead time to fill and they have to respond, they can quickly think of something interesting to say. Williams had done extensive research on the swimming competitions, but as cohost of the main broadcast, she would have to cover and comment on a range of sports. She'd be going in cold, with little more than her general knowledge of athletics to go on.

Williams agreed to step in. Since her first appearance would take place later that day, she had only four hours to prepare. Putting her two young children in her mother's care, she raced around the television studio, doing her best to coordinate her wardrobe and makeup and to run through the broadcast schedule with the network's production team. To help ease her nerves, she decided to write her opening remarks and read them off a teleprompter. She anticipated that once those first few minutes were behind her, she would get in the groove and be fine.

That evening, Williams was calm and in control as her male cohost welcomed her onto the show. But a moment later, when the lights came on and the cameras were live, disaster struck. Her cohost read the text on the teleprompter that she had prepared. She looked for any text that he had created, but there was none—the screen was blank.

For the next few moments, as over a million viewers looked on, Williams would somehow have to talk spontaneously about beach volleyball and the 100-meter hurdles race, events about which she knew next to nothing.

Williams's quandary was an extreme one—most of us never find ourselves on the world's stage having to test our skills the way she did. But as we've seen in this book, high-pressure spontaneous speaking opportunities arise every day, in a wide array of social contexts. Without warning, we are called to step up and express ourselves before colleagues, bosses, customers, family members, and even total strangers. Although our own fears and past experiences can make such moments feel daunting, they need not prevent us from thriving in the moment. No matter how affable, sociable, and facile with words we perceive ourselves to be, we can all become more comfortable and confident in the moment by employing the Think Faster, Talk Smarter method I've outlined as well as the context specific structures I've provided.

This method, as we've seen, has six steps:

First, we must acknowledge what we already know—that communication in general, and impromptu speaking in particular, is nerve wracking. We must create a personalized anxiety management plan to help address our jitters. [Calm]

Second, we must reflect on our approach to communication and how we judge ourselves and others, seeing these situations as opportunities for connection and collaboration. [Unlock]

Third, we must give ourselves permission to adopt new mindsets, take risks, and reenvision mistakes as missed takes. [Redefine]

Fourth, we must listen deeply to what others are saying (and perhaps not saying) while also tuning in to our own internal voice and intuition. [Listen]

Fifth, we must leverage story structure to make our ideas more intelligible, sharper, and compelling than they might otherwise have been. [Structure]

And sixth, we must focus audiences as much as possible on the essence of what we're saying, cultivating precision, relevance, accessibility, and concision. [Focus]

We can perform some of the work that these six steps require in the moment as we're speaking by adopting a range of helpful tactics. But more fundamentally, these six steps represent skills that we must cultivate over time as we prepare for spontaneous situations we think we're likely to have. Many people presume that speaking well when put on the spot requires natural talent—quick-wittedness or the gift of gab. While some of us certainly possess these talents, the real secret to spontaneous speaking is *practice* and *preparation*. All of us can become strong speakers in the moment if we put in the time, learn to break old habits, and exercise more deliberate choices. Paradoxically, we have to prepare in advance to do well in spontaneous situations, working hard on skills that we know will free us up to bring out our ideas and personalities to the fullest.

As when learning any new skill, it helps to reduce the pressure you put on yourself. You don't have to stress yourself out trying to master spontaneous communication all at once. Moreover, the very fact that you're focusing on improving yourself in this way is already worth celebrating. Most people either don't think about spontaneous speaking, or if they do, they aren't courageous enough to do anything about it. You are aware and brave, as evidenced by the fact that you picked up this book in the first place. I'm also willing to bet that you've already begun to make progress. Reading through this book and trying a few of its exercises has hopefully made you just a bit better at relaxing and communicating in impromptu situations.

I invite you during the weeks, months, and years ahead to continue to focus on spontaneous communication and practice the skills we've discussed. Try to put yourself into social situations where you can experiment with some of the skills and techniques. Don't test yourself in this way just once or occasionally—mindfully practice multiple times a week if you can. Consider taking an improvisational comedy class, even if you don't aspire to become the next cast member of *Saturday Night Live*. Join Toastmasters, listen to podcasts like mine, take online courses, and get feedback on your progress from trusted friends. This book is just a beginning, and it can serve to launch you on an ongoing process of growth and development as a communicator. I hope you'll return to this book often as you proceed in your efforts or need a refresher. As I think you'll find, once you start making progress, you'll see the value of thinking faster and talking smarter and feel energized to continue.

Becoming adept at spontaneous communication takes patience, commitment and grace, but as the people I coach and teach have found, the impact can be life changing.

Annabelle Williams is a great example. She didn't freeze up and wither under the pressure of having to communicate spontaneously in front of a live television audience. Because she had already spent years learning how to handle her anxieties, reframe communication tasks in helpful ways, and speak in a focused manner, she had the confidence to adapt quickly in this unexpected situation and make it through. Staying calm, she thought of a couple stray facts she happened to know about beach volleyball and the 100-meter hurdles race. Reframing this difficult moment as an opportunity to share these facts, she improvised some quick remarks. Then she transitioned the broadcast over to a live, on-the-ground interview and everything was fine—the moment had passed and she'd done well. She wound up serving as prime-time cohost for the final four nights of the Commonwealth Games broadcast, an experience that she found exhilarating and, as she put it, "brilliant."[1] Who knows where this success will take her next.

I'd like to close with a small story that holds a big place in my heart. When I got my first black belt, my sensei shook my hand and said, "Congratulations, you did very well. Now, let's get started." I thought that receiving a black belt was an enormous accomplishment, the culmination of a long period of study. In truth, it was just the first step—there was an infinite amount still to learn. Spontaneous communication is like this. Congratulations, you made it through this book. You know more about how to stay in the moment, project your personality, and communicate under the spotlight's glare.

Now, let's get started.*

---

* A great way to continue your learning is to visit the website you can find in appendix 2 a few pages from here.

APPENDIX 1

Structures for Use in Specific Situations

Practical Application	Possible Structure
Application #1: Small Talk	**What–So What–Now What:** Make an argument or point **(What)**; describe the significance of this information **(So What)**; suggest what your audience might do given their new knowledge **(Now What)**.
Application #2: Toasts	**WHAT:** Explain **w**hy are we here; share **h**ow are you connected; offer **a**necdotes and/or lessons you learned that relate to the person, group, or event you're commemorating; **t**hank the person, group, or event that you're commemorating and offer well-wishes.

Practical Application	Possible Structure
Application #3: **Pitching**	**Problem–Solution–Benefit:** Define a challenge, issue, pain point, or **problem** that you are addressing, one that your audience shares; present a **solution** to the problem, spelling out the specific steps, process/product, or method for remedying the problem; describe the **benefits** that adoption of your proposed solution will yield. **Bonus structure:** When pitching to obtain support from others for a new or growing business venture, complete the following **sentence starters:** **"What if you could . . ."** **"So that . . ."** **"For example . . ."** **"And that's not all . . ."**
Application #4: **Q&A**	**ADD: A**nswer the question in a single sentence. **D**etail an example that supports your answer. **D**escribe the benefits that explain why your answer is relevant to the asker.
Application #5: **Feedback**	**The 4 I's:** Provide **I**nformation. Explain the **I**mpact. Extend an **I**nvitation. Detail the **I**mplications.
Application #6: **Apologies**	**AAA: A**cknowledge the offending behavior and take responsibility for it; **a**ppreciate how your offense has impacted others. Detail how you will make **a**mends, specifying what action you will take or refrain from taking to remedy the situation or how your thinking will change.

APPENDIX 2

Web Page for New Material

To assist on your path to becoming a more confident and effective spontaneous communicator, I have created a Think Faster, Talk Smarter website that I will continually update with new ideas, tips, tools, and advice to help you along your way. You can expect to find articles and videos further detailing concepts covered in this book as well as others that extend and expand what I cover here. Just as I hope you return to this book over and over again for help when you need it, I encourage you to frequently check out this site.

Simply take your smartphone's camera and aim it at this QR code to open this helpful resource.

ACKNOWLEDGMENTS

This project originated in a cold call I received from Leah Trouwborst, who eventually got me to say "yes, and . . ." after a few "yes, maybes . . ." My agent Christy Fletcher and her team, especially Sarah Fuentes, played a critical role in helping me to arrive at "yes, and . . . ," and for that I am immensely grateful. Christy also taught me that "not yet" isn't just a growth mindset mantra but a great negotiation tactic. Our negotiations paid off because I got to work with the amazing Simon Element team, including Richard Rhorer, Michael Andersen, Elizabeth Breeden, Jessica Preeg, Nan Rittenhouse, Ingrid Carabulea, Clare Maurer, and my incredibly helpful, patient, and insightful editor, Leah Miller. Finally, I was very fortunate to collaborate with my writing sherpa and newfound friend Seth Schulman. This book is so much better because of Seth's expertise and experience, and so am I.

Many people helped me to gain the insights, awareness, and practical knowledge reflected in this book. First, I wish to thank all of my students, coaching clients, and podcast guests and listeners. I learn as much from you, if not more, than you learn from me. Thank you also to my draft readers: Lain Ehmann, David Paul Doyle, Bonnie Wright, Serene Wallace, and Clint Rosenthal. I appreciate each of you for taking the time to read these pages.

Next, I wish to express my appreciation to Adam Tobin, my Improvisationally Speaking coinstructor, friend, and mentor. Thank you,

Adam, for showing me the power of improv to improve communication and lives. I feel enormously grateful as well for my coteachers Kristin Hansen, Lauren Weinstein, Shawon Jackson, and Brendan Boyle and for the support and knowledge sharing I receive from J. D. Schramm, Allison Kluger, and Burt Alper. Thank you to the Graduate School of Business at Stanford and the Continuing Studies program for constantly encouraging me to innovate and create meaningful content for our students, and to the GSB deans who have supported my teaching, workshops, and podcast.

With regard to *Think Fast, Talk Smart: The Podcast,* I feel indebted to my amazing executive producer, Jenny Luna, and the entire GSB marketing communication team past and present, including Sorel Denholtz, Page Hetzel, Kelsey Doyle, Neil McPhedran, Cory Hall, Tricia Seibold, Sacha Ledan, Aileen Sato Chang, Michael Freedman, and Shana Lynch. Beyond the podcast, I also greatly appreciate the input and guidance of several Stanford authors, including Jennifer Aaker, Naomi Bagdonas, Bob Sutton, Tina Seelig, Jeremy Utley, Sarah Stein Greenburg, Carole Robin and Patricia Ryan Madson.

Richard Arioto, my sensei for more than forty years, has imparted lessons that continue to guide my life outside the martial arts school. I also thank Phil Zimbardo for showing me that teaching must be engaging for students and that research can be a creative art; my graduate school professors, who helped strengthen my conviction in the value of applied communication as a scholarly pursuit; and the friends and peers in my Book, Cooking, SINners, and Old Dudes Clubs and in Team Onagadori, all of whom provided much-needed input, distraction, support, and "therapy."

I would like to express my deep gratitude to my immediate and extended family. Thank you to my parents and to my brother for encouraging me as I pursued my dreams and for helping me to remember that we all must make mistakes in order to learn and grow. To my sons, thank you for your patience as well as your emotional and technical support. I'm grateful for your efforts to ensure that I don't say anything too embarrassing online.

To my wife, thank you so much for your continued love, encouragement, counseling, and advice. You graciously supported my book-writing "hobby." Thank you for reminding me not only to practice what I teach, especially when it comes to listening, but also to be patient with myself as I continue to hone my communication.

When it comes to developing our communication, we all do best when we take our time, give ourselves permission to take chances, and afford ourselves some grace when our experiments don't work out.

NOTES

INTRODUCTION

1. Christopher Ingraham, "America's Top Fears: Public Speaking, Heights and Bugs," *Washington Post*, October 30, 2014, https://www.washingtonpost.com/news/wonk/wp/2014/10/30/clowns-are-twice-as-scary-to-democrats-as-they-are-to-republicans/.

2. "Why Are Speakers 19% Less Confident in Impromtu Settings?," Quantified, September 13, 2016, https://www.quantified.ai/blog/why-are-speakers-19-less-confident-in-impromptu-settings/.

3. Verge, "Michael Bay CES Meltdown," YouTube video, 1:19, January 6, 2014, https://www.youtube.com/watch?v=23ypkgYO4Rc; Rory Carroll, "Michael Bay Walks Off CES Stage After Autocue Fails at Samsung TV Talk," *Guardian*, January 6, 2014, https://www.theguardian.com/film/2014/jan/07/michael-bay-walks-out-ces-samsung-presentation.

Chapter 1:
TAME THE ANXIETY BEAST

1. Research has found that anxiety can "compromise performance on cognitively demanding tasks and lead people to perform below their ability." It does that by sapping working memory and taxing parts of your brain you use for thinking tasks. See Erin A. Maloney, Jason R. Sattizahn, and Sian L. Beilock, "Anxiety and Cognition," *WIREs Cognitive Science* 5, no. 4 (July/August 2014): 403–11, https://doi.org/10.1002/wcs.1299.

2. Kenneth Savitsky and Thomas Gilovich, "The Illusion of Transparency and the Alleviation of Speech Anxiety," *Journal of Experi-*

mental Social Psychology 39, no. 6 (November 2003): 619, https://doi.org/10.1016/S0022-1031(03)00056-8.

3. Alyson Meister and Maude Lavanchy, "The Science of Choking Under Pressure," *Harvard Business Review*, April 7, 2022, https://hbr.org/2022/04/the-science-of-choking-under-pressure. For more on the mechanisms of choking under pressure, see Marcus S. Decaro et al., "Choking Under Pressure: Multiple Routes to Skill Failure," *Journal of Experimental Psychology* 140, no. 3, 390–406, https://doi.org/10.1037/a0023466.

4. Ann Pietrangelo, "What the Yerkes-Dodson Law Says About Stress and Performance," Healthline, October 22, 2020, https://www.healthline.com/health/yerkes-dodson-law. See also Nick Morgan, "Are You Anxious? What Are the Uses of Anxiety, if Any?" Public Words, May 17, 2022, https://publicwords.com/2022/05/17/are-you-anxious-what-are-the-uses-of-anxiety-if-any/.

5. Elizabeth D. Kirby et al., "Acute Stress Enhances Adult Rat Hippocampal Neurogenesis and Activation of Newborn Neurons via Secreted Astrocytic FGF2," *eLife* 2: e00362. For a summary of this research, see Robert Sanders, "Researchers Find Out Why Some Stress Is Good for You," *Berkeley News*, April 16, 2013, https://news.berkeley.edu/2013/04/16/researchers-find-out-why-some-stress-is-good-for-you/.

6. Scholars have devised similar classification schemes for public speaking anxiety. See Graham D. Bodie, "A Racing Heart, Rattling Knees, and Ruminative Thoughts: Defining Explaining, and Treating Public Speaking Anxiety, *Communication Education* 59, no. 1 (2010): 70–105, https://doi.org/10.1080/03634520903443849.

7. Others recommend this as well. See Alyson Meister and Maude Lavanchy, "The Science of Choking Under Pressure," *Harvard Business Review*, April 7, 2022, https://hbr.org/2022/04/the-science-of-choking-under-pressure.

8. S. Christian Wheeler (StrataCom Professor of Management and Professor of Marketing at Stanford Graduate School of Business), interview with the author, June 7, 2022.

9. *The Brady Bunch*, season 5, episode 15, "The Driver's Seat," directed by Jack Arnold, aired January 11, 1974.

10. Alison Wood Brooks, "Get Excited: Reappraising Pre-Performance Anxiety as Excitement," *Journal of Experimental Psychology: General* 143, no. 1 (2013), DOI:10.1037/a0035325.

11. Andrew Huberman, interview with Matt Abrahams, "Hacking Your Speaking Anxiety: How Lessons from Neuroscience Can Help You Communicate Confidently," *Think Fast, Talk Smart*, podcast, May 14, 2021, https://www.gsb.stanford.edu/insights /hacking-your-speaking-anxiety-how-lessons-neuroscience-can -help-you-communicate.

12. Huberman, "Hacking Your Speaking Anxiety."

13. We can use mantras for other purposes as well, such as to become more inclusive and welcoming. See Deborah Gruenfeld, "Using a Mantra to Be a More Inclusive Leader," *Harvard Business Review*, February 24, 2022, https://hbr.org/2022/02/using-a-mantra-to -be-a-more-inclusive-leader.

14. Thomas Gilovich et al., "The Spotlight Effect Revisited: Overesti- mating the Manifest Variability of Our Actions and Appearance," *Journal of Experimental Social Psychology* 38, no. 1 (January 2002): 93–99, https://www.sciencedirect.com/science/article/abs/pii /S0022103101914908.

Chapter 2:
MAXIMIZE MEDIOCRITY

1. Keith Johnstone, *Impro: Improvisation and the Theatre* (New York: Routledge, 1987).

2. Federica Scarpina and Sofia Tagini, "The Stroop Color and Word Test," *Frontiers in Psychology* 8, article 557 (April 2017), https:// doi.org/10.3389/fpsyg.2017.00557.

3. For more on Cognitive Load Theory, see Fred Paas and Jeroen J. G. van Merriënboer, "Cognitive-Load Theory: Methods to Manage Working Memory Load in the Learning of Complex Tasks," *Current Directions in Psychological Science* 29, no. 4 (July 8, 2020), https://doi.org/10.1177/0963721420922183; George Christodoulides, "Effects of Cognitive Load on Speech Produc- tion and Perception" (PhD diss., Catholic University of Louvain, 2016), https://www.afcp-parole.org/doc/theses/these_GC16.pdf;

Paul A. Kirschner, "Cognitive Load Theory: Implications of Cognitive Load Theory on the Design of Learning," *Learning and Instruction* 12, no. 1 (February 2002): 1–10; and "What to Do When Cognitive Overload Threatens Your Productivity," Atlassian.com, downloaded October 24, 2022, https://www.atlassian.com/blog/productivity/cognitive-overload.

4. For more on heuristics, see Steve Dale, "Heuristics and Biases: The Science of Decision-Making," *Business Information Review* 32, no. 2 (2015): 93–99, https://doi.org/10.1177/0266382115592536, and Fatima M. Albar and Antonie J. Jetter, "Heuristics in Decision Making," *Proceedings of Portland International Conference on Management of Engineering & Technology* (2009): 578–84, DOI:10.1109/PICMET.2009.5262123. For the role heuristics play in alleviating cognitive load, see Justin Sentz and Jill Stefaniak, "Instructional Heuristics for the Use of Worked Examples to Manage Instructional Designers' Cognitive Load while Problem-Solving," *TechTrends* 63 (2019), https://doi.org/10.1007/s11528-018-0348-8.

5. Susan Weinschenk, "The Power of the Word 'Because' to Get People to Do Stuff," *Psychology Today*, October 15, 2013, https://www.psychologytoday.com/us/blog/brain-wise/201310/the-power-the-word-because-get-people-do-stuff.

6. My account of this anecdote draws on Tina Seelig, "Tina Seelig: Classroom Experiments in Entrepreneurship," YouTube video, 6:11, May 31, 2011, https://www.youtube.com/watch?v=VVgIX0s1wY8.

7. Maura Cass and Owen Sanderson, "To Transform Your Industry, Look at Someone Else's," IDEO, May 22, 2019, https://www.ideo.com/journal/to-transform-your-industry-look-at-someone-elses.

8. My first memory of the "dare to be dull" phrase came from Tina Fey's book *Bossypants*. We often refer to this concept in the Improvisationally Speaking class I coteach to help our students better understand that they needn't feel pressure to always be "on" and contribute something amazing to their interactions. See Tina Fey, *Bossypants* (New York: Little, Brown and Company, 2011).

9. Matt Abrahams, "Speaking without a Net: How to Master Impromptu Communication," *Stanford Business*, January 17, 2020,

https://www.gsb.stanford.edu/insights/speaking-without-net-how
-master-impromptu-communication. Klein was referencing the
teachings of another master improviser, Keith Johnstone.

10. Matt Abrahams, "Managing in the Moment: How to Get Comfortable with Being Uncomfortable," *Stanford Business*, August 28,
2020, https://www.gsb.stanford.edu/insights/managing-moment
-how-get-comfortable-being-uncomfortable.

11. See Matt Abrahams, "The Trick to Public Speaking Is to Stop
Memorizing," Quartz, updated July 20, 2022, https://qz.com
/work/1642074/the-trick-to-public-speaking-is-to-stop-memoriz
ing/.

12. "Our Mission," FLS Academy, accessed November 28, 2022,
https://fls.academy/our-mission.

13. Anthony Veneziale, "'Stumbling Towards Intimacy': An Improvised TED Talk," YouTube video, 11:02, https://www.ted.com
/talks/anthony_veneziale_stumbling_towards_intimacy_an_im
provised_ted_talk.

14. Vivek Venugopal (vice president of sales at Mindless Inc.), interview with the author, May 20, 2022.

15. Improvisation expert Adam Tobin made similar points during
his appearance on my podcast. See Matt Abrahams, "Speaking
without a Net: How to Master Impromptu Communication,"
Stanford Business, January 17, 2020, https://www.gsb.stanford.edu
/insights/speaking-without-net-how-master-impromptu-commu
nication.

Chapter 3:
MIND YOUR MINDSET

1. Hear Dan's account of his experience on Matt Abrahams, "Speaking without a Net: How to Master Impromptu Communication,"
Stanford Business, January 17, 2020, https://www.gsb.stanford
.edu/insights/speaking-without-net-how-master-impromptu-com
munication.

2. Dan Klein (improvisation expert and lecturer at Stanford Graduate School of Business), interview with the author, June 19, 2022.

3. Trevor Wallace, interview with the author, June 22, 2022.

4. Clay Drinko, "Is the 'Yes, And' Improv Rule a Rule for Life?," *Play Your Way Sane* (blog), September 2, 2020, https://www.playyour waysane.com/blog/is-the-yes-and-improv-rule-a-rule-for-life

5. Craig O. Stewart et al., "Growth Mindset: Associations with Apprehension, Self-Perceived Competence, and Beliefs about Public Speaking," *Basic Communication Course Annual* 31, no. 6 (2019), https://ecommons.udayton.edu/bcca/vol31/iss1/6.

6. Carol Dweck, *Mindset: The New Psychology of Success* (New York: Ballantine Books, 2016); "The Power of Believing That You Can Improve," TEDxNorrkoping Video, 10:11, https://www.ted.com/talks/carol_dweck_the_power_of_believing_that_you_can_improve. I also draw in this section on the summary of Dweck's work provided in "Carol Dweck: A Summary of Growth and Fixed Mindsets," *fs* (blog), https://fs.blog/carol-dweck-mindset/.

7. Jennifer Aaker, "Step by Step: Think of Goals as Part of the Journey, Not the Destination," Character Lab, May 22, 2022, https://characterlab.org/tips-of-the-week/step-by-step/.

8. Szu-chi Huang and Jennifer Aaker, "It's the Journey, Not the Destination: How Metaphor Drives Growth After Goal Attainment," *American Psychological Association* 117, no. 4 (2019): 697–720, https://doi.org/10.1037/pspa0000164.

9. Patricia Ryan Madson (improvisation expert and professor emerita at Stanford University), interview with the author, May 27, 2022.

10. Patricia Madson, email correspondence with the author, June 19, 2022.

11. Kathy Bonanno, interview with the author, June 17, 2022.

12. Kelly Leonard, *Yes, And: How Improvisation Reverses "No, But" Thinking and Improves Creativity and Collaboration* (New York: Harper Business, 2015).

13. Patricia Ryan Madson (improvisation expert and professor emerita at Stanford University), interview with the author, June 12, 2022. Madson tells this story in her book *Improv Wisdom: Don't Prepare, Just Show Up* (New York: Bell Tower, 2005).

14. Michael Kruse, "The Next Play: Over 42 Years, Mike Krzyzewski Sustained Excellence by Looking Ahead," *Duke Magazine*, March 16, 2022, https://alumni.duke.edu/magazine/articles/next-play.
15. Kruse, "The Next Play."
16. See, for instance, Maitti Showhopper, "New Choice," Improwiki, updated September 23, 2015, https://improwiki.com/en/wiki/improv/new_choice.
17. Tie Kim (CFO of the California Health Care Foundation), interview with the author, May 27, 2022.
18. Jade Panugan, "'The Story of the Chinese Farmer' by Alan Watts," Craftdeology, https://www.craftdeology.com/the-story-of-the-chinese-farmer-by-alan-watts/.

Chapter 4:
DON'T JUST DO SOMETHING . . . STAND THERE!
1. Fred Dust, *Making Conversation: Seven Essential Elements of Meaningful Communication* (New York: HarperBusiness, 2020).
2. Fred Dust (former senior partner and global managing director at IDEO), interview with the author, June 17, 2022.
3. Ari Fleischer (former White House press secretary in the administration of George W. Bush), interview with the author, June 17, 2022.
4. Matt Abrahams, "Speaking without a Net: How to Master Impromptu Communication," *Stanford Business*, January 17, 2020, https://www.gsb.stanford.edu/insights/speaking-without-net-how-master-impromptu-communication.
5. Guy Itzchakov and Avraham N. (Avi) Kluger, "The Power of Listening in Helping People Change," *Harvard Business Review*, May 17, 2018, https://hbr.org/2018/05/the-power-of-listening-in-helping-people-change.
6. For more on business card etiquette in Japan, see "Business Card Etiquette in Japan—How to Exchange Business Cards," Japan Living Guide, June 21, 2021, https://www.japanlivingguide.net/business/business-in-japan/japan-business-card-etiquette/.
7. Collins Dobbs and Matt Abrahams, "Space, Pace, and Grace: How to Handle Challenging Conversations," *Stanford Business*,

October 15, 2021, https://www.gsb.stanford.edu/insights/space -pace-grace-how-handle-challenging-conversations.

8. Debra Schifrin and Matt Abrahams, "Question Everything: Why Curiosity Is Communication's Secret Weapon," *Stanford Business*, March 12, 2021, https://www.gsb.stanford.edu/insights/question -everything-why-curiosity-communications-secret-weapon.

9. Guy Itzchakov and Avraham N. (Avi) Kluger, "The Power of Listening in Helping People Change," *Harvard Business Review*, May 17, 2018, https://hbr.org/2018/05/the-power-of-listening-in -helping-people-change.

10. Tania Israel, "How to Listen—Really Listen—to Someone You Don't Agree With," *Ideas.Ted*, October 12, 2020, https://ideas.ted .com/how-to-listen-really-listen-to-someone-you-dont-agree-with/.

11. Guy Itzchakov (lecturer at the Faculty of Business Administration at the University of Haifa in Israel), interview with the author, June 24, 2022.

12. Bob Baxley (former senior design executive at Apple, Pinterest, and Yahoo), interview with the author, June 23, 2022.

13. Matt Abrahams, "Speaking without a Net: How to Master Im-promptu Communication," *Stanford Business*, January 17, 2020, https://www.gsb.stanford.edu/insights/speaking-without-net -how-master-impromptu-communication.

14. Matt Abrahams, "Building Successful Relationships: How to Effec-tively Communicate in Your Professional and Personal Life," *Stan-ford Business*, February 18, 2021, https://www.gsb.stanford.edu /insights/building-successful-relationships-how-effectively-com municate-your-professional-personal.

15. Kim Zetter, "Robin Williams Saves the Day at TED When Tech Fails," *Wired*, February 28, 2008, https://www.wired.com /2008/02/robin-williams/. For a video of some of Williams's appearance, see Garr Reynolds, "Robin Williams on the TED Stage," Presentation Zen, August 2014, https://www.presentation zen.com/presentationzen/2014/08/robin-williams-on-the-ted -stage.html.

Chapter 5:

STRUCTURE YOUR SPONTANEITY

1. Meghan Talarowski (play designer and founder of Studio Ludo), interview with the author, July 29, 2022.

2. Sue Stanley (senior instructional designer at Toastmasters International), interview with the author, June 29, 2022.

3. "Music 101: What Is Song Structure?" *Masterclass*, August 9, 2021, https://www.masterclass.com/articles/music-101-what-is-song-structure.

4. On the ABDCE structure, see for instance Avani Pandya, "Understanding the ABDCE Plot Structure (with Some Context on Mentoring a Course)," LinkedIn, October 21, 2021, https://www.linkedin.com/pulse/understanding-abdce-plot-structure-some-context-mentoring-pandya/.

5. David Labaree (professor of education at Stanford University), interview with the author, August 2, 2022.

6. Dalmeet Singh Chawla, "To Remember, the Brain Must Actively Forget," *Quanta*, July 24, 2018, https://www.quantamagazine.org/to-remember-the-brain-must-actively-forget-20180724/.

7. Rachel Barclay, "Your Memory Is Unreliable, and Science Could Make It More So," Healthline, September 13, 2013, https://www.healthline.com/health-news/mental-memory-is-unreliable-and-it-could-be-worse-091313.

8. "Brains Love Stories: How Leveraging Neuroscience Can Capture People's Emotions," *Stanford Business*, September 2, 2021, https://www.gsb.stanford.edu/insights/brains-love-stories-how-leveraging-neuroscience-can-capture-peoples-emotions.

9. "Jennifer Aaker—Persuasion and the Power of Story," Future of Storytelling video, 5:08, https://futureofstorytelling.org/video/jennifer-aaker-the-power-of-story.

10. Frank Longo (professor of medicine and neurosurgery at Stanford University), interview with the author, July 21, 2022.

11. Jennifer Aaker, "Faculty Profile," *Stanford Business*, accessed October 4, 2022, https://www.gsb.stanford.edu/faculty-research/faculty/jennifer-aaker; "Jennifer Aaker—Persuasion and the Power of Story."

12. "Jennifer Aaker—Persuasion and the Power of Story."

13. Raymond Nasr (former director of executive communications at Google), interview with the author, June 8, 2022.

14. Myka Carroll, *New York City for Dummies* (Hoboken, NJ: Wiley, 2010).

15. Myka Carroll (editorial director of the For Dummies series and author of *New York City for Dummies*), email correspondence on December 19, 2022.

16. Josef Parvizi (professor of neurology at Stanford University), interview with the author, August 5, 2022.

17. James Whittington (improvisation and theater teacher and director at Second City), email correspondence with the author, July 12, 2022.

18. I draw here on the following: Matt Button, "Impromptu Speaking Techniques," Mattbutton.com, February 23, 2019, https://www.mattbutton.com/2019/02/23/impromptu-speaking-techniques/; Leah, "4 Ways Structure Can Improve Your Communication," Userlike, September 4, 2019, https://www.userlike.com/en/blog/talk-with-structure; and "How to Use the STAR Interview Technique in Interviews," Indeed, updated September 23, 2022, https://uk.indeed.com/career-advice/interviewing/star-technique.

19. These tools are available at, respectively, "Table Topics," Virtual Speech, accessed October 4, 2022, https://virtualspeech.com/tools/table-topics and "Interview Warmup," Google (certificate), accessed October 4, 2022, https://grow.google/certificates/interview-warmup/.

20. Karen Dunn (partner at the law firm Paul, Weiss, Rifkind, Wharton & Garrison and an expert on presidential debate preparation), interview with the author, June 6, 2022.

21. Raymond Nasr (former director of executive communications at Google), interview with the author, June 8, 2022.

22. Andrew Bright, "The Story Spine," Panic Squad Improv Comedy, accessed October 4, 2022, https://careynieuwhof.com/wp-content/uploads/2016/08/Improv-Story-Spine.pdf.

Chapter 6:

THE F-WORD OF SPONTANEOUS SPEAKING

1. Joshua VanDeBrake, "Steve Jobs' Blueprint for Revolutionary Marketing," *Better Marketing*, August 24, 2019, https://better marketing.pub/steve-jobs-blueprint-for-revolutionary-marketing -b88ec38f335; Vejay Anand, "Iconic Ads: iPod—Thousand Songs in Your Pocket," Only Kutts, July 30, 2021, https://onlykutts .com/index.php/2021/07/30/ipod-a-thousand-songs-in-your -pocket/.

2. Baba Shiv, interview with Matt Abrahams, "Feelings First: How Emotion Shapes Our Communication, Decisions, and Experiences," *Think Fast, Talk Smart*, podcast, November 20, 2020, https://www.gsb.stanford.edu/insights/feelings-first-how -emotion-shapes-communication-decisions-experiences.

3. Scott Magids, Alan Zorfas, and Daniel Leemon, "The New Science of Customer Emotions," *Harvard Business Review* (November 2015), https://hbr.org/2015/11/the-new-science-of-customer -emotions. Research has also found that political advertisements "motivate and persuade voters by appealing to emotions." See Youn-Kyung Kim and Pauline Sullivan, "Emotional Branding Speaks to Consumers' Heart: The Case of Fashion Brands," *Fashion and Textiles* 6, no. 2 (February 2019), https://doi.org/10.1186 /s40691-018-0164-y.

4. Jim Koch, *Quench Your Own Thirst: Business Lessons Learned over a Beer or Two* (New York: Flatiron Books, 2016), 72–74.

5. I first encountered this term in chapter 2 of Chip and Dan Heath's book *Made to Stick: Why Some Ideas Survive and Others Die* (New York: Random House, 2007): 31–32.

6. Carmine Gallo, "Neuroscience Proves You Should Follow TED's 18-Minute Rule to Win Your Pitch," *Inc.*, accessed October 6, 2022, https://www.inc.com/carmine-gallo/why-your-next-pitch-should -follow-teds-18-minute-rule.html.

7. "Glossary of Demographic Terms," PRB, accessed October 6, 2022, https://www.prb.org/resources/glossary/.

8. Justin Kestler (vice president of product and operations at Course Hero), interview with the author, August 4, 2022.

9. Anthony Dalby (designer at the LEGO Group), interview with the author, August 10, 2022.

10. For more on such strategies, see Matt Abrahams, "Hit the Mark: Make Complex Ideas Understandable," *Stanford Business*, March 29, 2018, https://www.gsb.stanford.edu/insights/hit-mark -make-complex-ideas-understandable.

11. I am indebted to Zakary Tormala for this point. For background, please see Richard E. Petty et al., "Motivation to Think and Order Effects in Persuasion: The Moderating Role of Chunking," *Personality and Social Psychology Bulletin* 27, no. 3 (March 2001): 332–44, DOI:10.1177/0146167201273007.

12. Josef Parvizi (professor of neurology at Stanford University), interview with the author, August 5, 2022.

13. "About," Six Word Stories, December 28, 2008, http://www.six wordstories.net/about/.

14. "Largest Companies by Market Cap," Companies Market Cap, accessed October 6, 2022, https://companiesmarketcap.com/.

15. Raymond Nasr (former director of executive communications at Google), interview with the author, June 8, 2022.

16. "Maximize Access to Information," Google, accessed October 4, 2022, https://www.google.com/search/howsearchworks/our-approach/.

Application #1:
GOING BIG ON SMALL TALK

1. The more we disclose about ourselves, the more others disclose as well. See Elizabeth Bernstein, "Have Better Conversations with Friends—or Anyone," *Wall Street Journal*, July 26, 2022, https:// www.wsj.com/articles/have-better-conversations-with-friendsor -anyone-11658845993.

2. Scholars have described conversations in terms of turn-taking. See Michael Yeomans et al., "The Conversational Circumplex: Identifying, Prioritizing, and Pursuing Informational and Relational Motives in Conversation," *Current Opinion in Psychology* 44 (2022): 293–302, https://doi.org/10.1016/j.copsyc.2021.10.001.

3. Celeste Headlee, "Why We Should All Stop Saying 'I Know Exactly How You Feel,'" *Ideas.Ted*, September 21, 2017, https://ideas.ted .com/why-we-should-all-stop-saying-i-know-exactly-how-you-feel/.

4. Email correspondence with Rachel Greenwald, August 12, 2022, and December 2, 2022.

5. Ibid.

6. Michael Yeoman et al., "Conversational Receptiveness: Improving Engagement with Opposing Views," *Organizational Behavior and Human Decision Processes* 160 (September 2020): 131–48, https:// doi.org/10.1016/j.obhdp.2020.03.011.

Application #3:
MAKE THAT (IM)PERFECT PITCH

1. Examples include Robert B. Cialdini, *Influence* (New York: Collins, 2007); Chip Heath and Dan Health, *Switch: How to Change Things When Change Is Hard* (New York: Broadway Books, 2010); and Zoe Chance, *Influence Is Your Superpower: The Science of Winning Hearts, Sparking Change, and Making Good Things Happen* (New York: Random House, 2022).

2. Andy Raskin, "Want a Better Pitch?" Medium, July 13, 2015, https://medium.com/firm-narrative/want-a-better-pitch-watch -this-328b95c2fd0b.

3. See J. L. Freedman and S. C. Fraser, "Compliance without Pressure: The Foot-in-the-Door Technique," *Journal of Personality and Social Psychology* 4, no. 2 (1966): 195–202.

4. In this and the following tip, I draw on material in my book *Speaking Up without Freaking Out: 50 Techniques for Confident and Compelling Presenting* (Dubuque, IA: Kendall Hunt, 2016).

5. For more on addressing the obstacles, see Andy Raskin, "The Greatest Sales Deck I've Ever Seen," Medium, September 15, 2016, https://medium.com/the-mission/the-greatest-sales-deck -ive-ever-seen-4f4ef3391ba0.

Application #4:

ROCKING THE Q&A

1. See also the appendix of my book *Speaking Up without Freaking Out: 50 Techniques for Confident and Compelling Presenting* (Dubuque, IA: Kendall Hunt, 2016). Some of this content originally appeared there as well as in video trainings and other handouts I've created.

Application #5:

FEEDBACK THAT DOESN'T FLOP

1. Ruben Nieves (head men's coach at Stanford University, head women's coach at California State University, Fresno, and director of training at the Positive Coaching Alliance), interview with the author, May 31, 2022.
2. Therese Huston, "Giving Critical Feedback Is Even Harder Remotely," *Harvard Business Review,* January 26, 2021, https://hbr .org/2021/01/giving-critical-feedback-is-even-harder-remotely.

Application #6:

THE SECRETS TO SAYING WE'RE SORRY

1. John Baldoni, "What John Wayne Got Wrong About Apologizing," *Forbes,* April 3, 2019, https://www.forbes.com/sites/john baldoni/2019/04/03/what-john-wayne-got-wrong-about-apolo gizing/.
2. In preparing this section, I've drawn heavily on Lolly Daskol, "The Right and Wrong Way to Apologize and Why It Matters," *Inc.,* November 27, 2017, https://www.inc.com/lolly-daskal/the-right -wrong-way-to-apologize-why-it-matters.html.

EPILOGUE

1. Annabelle Williams, "Reflecting on the past couple of weeks," LinkedIn, accessed October 6, 2022, https://www.linkedin.com /posts/annabellewilliams_community-mentorship-sponsorship -activity-6964726246865846272-acYp/.

INDEX

J

jargon, 123–124, 126, 127, 156

jazz musicians, 95

job interviews

  ADD structure used for, 180

  anxiety management plan (AMP)
    used for, 31–32

  author's experience with, 17–18

  direct answers to questions in, 174

  having some key lines and talking
    points ready for, 50

  hostile audiences in, 58

  "peeling-back-the-onion" question
    at, 17–18

  Problem-Solution-Benefit structure
    for, 169–170

  setting boundaries in, 177

  What-So What-Now What structure
    for, 106

Jobs, Steve, 7, 113–114

Johnston, Steve, 45, 66

jokes, 90

journaling, 108–109

judging others/judgment from others,
  67, 89, 183

judging ourselves, 5, 43–44, 45, 47, 55

K

Kahneman, Daniel, 116

Kestler, Justin, 125, 127

Kim, Tie, 69

King, Martin Luther Jr., 99

Klein, Dan, 45, 56–57

Koch, Jim, 118

Kramon, Glenn, 130

L

Labaree, David, 98

Langer, Ellen, 37

language

  adjusting our use of, 49–50

  communicating with someone who
    has a language different from
    your, 201–202

  use of complex, 124

laying off employees, finding upsides
  in, 71–73

learning

  failures and mistakes as part of, 47,
    48, 60

  with a growth mindset, 59–60

LEGO, 126

LikeSo, 26

listen(ing), 75–92, 207

  benefits of, 77–79

  Drill It exercises on, 91–92

  example of, 75–77

  failure to, 79–80

  making small talk conversations
    about others by, 140

  making space for reflection while,
    84–87

  mindset, 82–83

  with more intent, 82

  nonverbal communication and, 82

  to our inner voice, 87–90

  Pace, Space, and Grace framework
    for, 80–90

  the power of, 77–78

  slowing pace of speaking for, 81–83

  why we miss opportunities for, 77

  "Yes, and . . . " posture and, 66

lists, 96

LitCharts, 125, 127

literature, study guides on, 125–126

Longo, Frank, 100

lost, trying to get, 56–57

M

Madson, Patricia Ryan, 61–62, 63,
  67–68

Making Conversation (Dust), 75

mantras, 23, 27, 29, 31, 60, 81

martial arts, 47–48

masculine terminology, 196, 197

"maybe," 70

mediocrity, perfectionism *versus*
  striving for, 35–36

memorizing what we will say, 8, 50–51,
  52, 110

INDEX

speaker and audience with,
99–101
mental shortcuts. *See* heuristics
(mental shortcuts)
mindfulness, 19–21, 27
Mindless, Inc., 45, 53, 54
mindset(s), 206
definition, 58
from dwelling on what happened to
"next play," 67–70
fixed, 59
growth, 59–60, 72
listening, 82–83
"next play," 68–70
reframing threat from audience, 58
to see impromptu interactions as
opportunities, 57
from thinking about you to thinking
about your audience, 61–64
from "yes, but . . . " to "yes, and . . .
," 64–67
Miranda, Lin-Manuel, 53
missed-takes, 46–48
mission statement, Google, 131
mistakes
embracing, 46–47, 52
not dwelling or ruminating on your,
67–68
reframed as missed-takes, 47–48
mixers, 138–139, 148, 181
movement(s)
dissipating shakiness with, 22
slowing down, 21, 27
Mrzyzewski, Mike (Coach K), 68
music
"1,000 songs in your pocket" phrase,
113–114
structure in, 95, 96
Musk, Elon, 163

N

narrative/story structure. *See*
structure(s)
Nasr, Raymond, 100, 101, 111, 131

negative comments, 144
negative issues, in Q&As, 175
negative self-talk, 19, 23
negative thoughts and feelings, 19–20
New Choice (game), 69
"next play" mindset, 68–70
Nieves, Ruben, 188
nonverbal communication, 82, 83
"not yet" attitude, 60

O

Obama, Michelle, 7
obstacles, addressing in pitches,
167–168
offending others, avoiding in small
talk, 146–147
onion, interview question on peeling
back the, 17–18, 31–32
online tools, 108
open-ended questions, 143
opportunity(ies)
to enhance the lives of others, 61–62
for learning, with a growth mindset,
59–60
by listening, 77–79
with Q&As, 172–173
reframing spontaneous
communication as an, 57
seizing as it arises, 68–69
Orai, 26
"orchestra conductor" approach, at
question-and-answer sessions,
178–179
original, saying something, 45
outlines, 51

P

pace, slowing down your, 81–83
Pace, Space, and Grace framework,
80–90
Page, Larry, 131
paraphrasing, 85–86, 91, 144, 146
listening and, 85, 86
practicing, 91
during small talk, 144, 146

238

ABOUT THE AUTHOR

Matt Abrahams is a leading expert in the field of communication. As a lecturer in organizational behavior at Stanford University's Graduate School of Business, he teaches popular classes in strategic communication and effective virtual presenting and has received the school's Alumni Teaching Award. Matt also teaches public speaking and coteaches Improvisationally Speaking in the Stanford Continuing Studies program.

When he isn't teaching, Matt is a highly sought-after keynote speaker and communications consultant and coach. He has helped numerous presenters prepare for high-stakes talks, including IPO road shows, Nobel Prize award presentations, and appearances at TED and the World Economic Forum. His online talks garner millions of views and he hosts the popular award-winning podcast *Think Fast, Talk Smart: The Podcast.* His book *Speaking Up without Freaking Out: 50 Techniques for Confident and Compelling Presenting* has helped a wide audience manage speaking anxiety and present more confidently and authentically.

To relax and rejuvenate, Matt enjoys hiking with his wife, talking and watching sports with his kids, hanging with his friends, and being continually humbled at his karate dojo.